Alaska

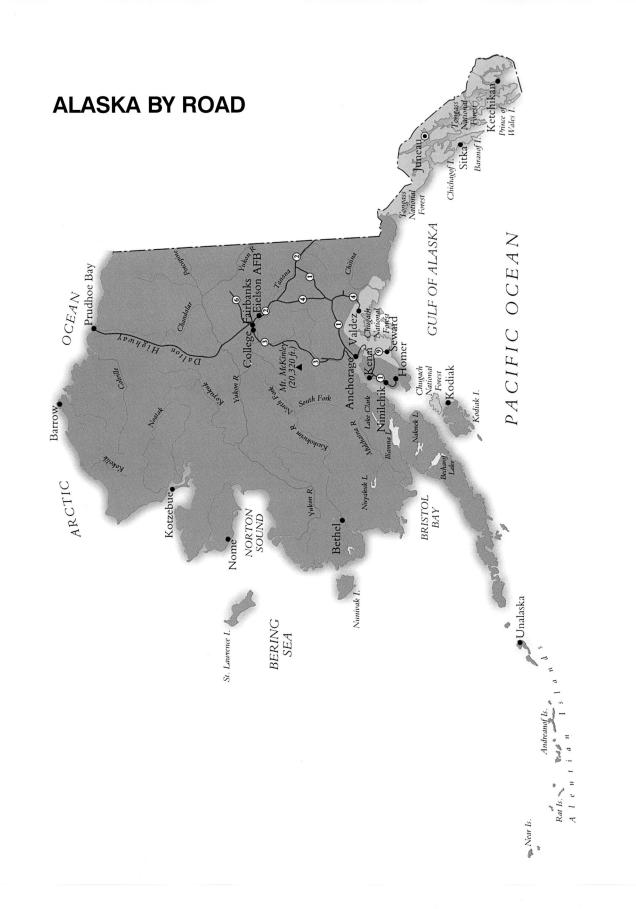

ALASKA BY ROAD

Celebrate the States

Alaska

Rebecca Stefoff

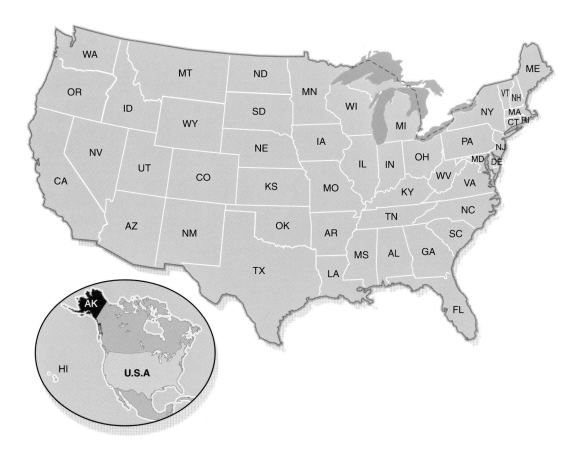

Marshall Cavendish
Benchmark
New York

Marshall Cavendish Benchmark
99 White Plains Road
Tarrytown, NY 10591-9001
www.marshallcavendish.us

Library of Congress Cataloging-in-Publication Data
Stefoff, Rebecca, 1951–
Alaska / by Rebecca Stefoff.—2nd ed.
p. cm.—(Celebrate the states)
Summary: "Provides comprehensive information on the geography, history, wildlife, governmental struc-
ture, economy, cultural diversity, peoples, religion, and landmarks of Alaska"—Provided by publisher.
Includes bibliographical references and index.
ISBN-13: 978-0-7614-2153-5
ISBN-10: 0-7614-2153-X
Alaska—Juvenile literature. I. Title. II. Series.
F904.3.S76 2006
979.8—dc222005027082

Editor: Christine Florie
Editorial Director: Michelle Bisson
Art Director: Anahid Hamparian
Series Designer: Adam Mietlowski
Photo research by Candlepants Incorporated

The photographs in this book are used by permission and through the courtesy of; *Corbis:*
Paul A. Souders, 8, 16, 128; Neil Rabinowitz, 11, 102; 13, 42, 43, 47, 49, 129,131, 133; David
Muench, 15; Jack Fields, 17; Greg Probst, 18; Brian Leng, 23; Joshua Strang, 27; Joe McDonald, 30;
Karen Kasmauski, 50; Natalie Fobes, 51; Roy Corral, 54; Peter Guttman, 58; Catherine Karnow, 63;
Caroline Penn, 65; Galen Rowell, 66 (low); Alison Wright, 66 (top); Troy Wayrynen/Columbian/
NewSport, 70; Tom Bean, 79, 103; Joseph Sohm/Chromosohm Inc. 81; Les Stone, 83; Lowell Georgia,
84; Pat O'Hara, 88, 101; Kevin Fleming, 91, 95, 100; Vince Streano, 97; Terry W. Eggers, 104;
Wolfgang Kaehler, 106; Frans Lanting, 136. *© 2005, AlaskaStock.com:* Jim D. Barr, 19, 61; Patrick
Endres, 21; Chris Arend & Tom Soucek, 26; Michael Jones, 29, 98; Michael DeYoung, 31, 118; John
Hyde, 32; Chris Arernd, 68, 93, 123, back cover; Don Pitcher, 86, 90; John Warden, 92; Chlaus
Lotscher, 109; Jeff Schultz, 112; Doug Lindstrand, 115 (top); Ernest Manewal, 115 (lower); Bill
Watkins, 119; Clark James Mishler, 125. *Anchorage Museum of History and Art:* Untitled Wrangell
Indian Villageca 1900 by Theodore J. Richardson, 34; Seal Hunters, Belmoore Browne, 38. *Bridgeman
Art Library:* Private Collection, 36; Bibliotheque des Arts Decoratifs, Paris, France, Archives Charmet,
37. *Alaska State Library:* 41 (top); Centennial Collection, 41 (low). *AP Wide World Photos:*
Joe Marquette, 74; Charles Mason, 77. *© Ken Graham/Accent Alaska:* 72.

Printed in China
1 3 5 6 4 2

Contents

Alaska Is . . .   6

Chapter One   9
Geography: The Great Land
The Biggest State ▪ Five Regions ▪ Rain, Snow, and Wind ▪ It's Getting Warmer ▪
Day and Night ▪ Wild Alaska ▪ Where the People Are

Chapter Two   35
History: The Making of Alaska
The First Alaskans ▪ Russian Alaska ▪ The United States Takes Over ▪ War
and Statehood ▪ The Rush for Liquid Gold ▪ Into the Twenty-first Century

Chapter Three   55
People: Life in the Big Beyond
Native Alaska ▪ Ethnic and Cultural Diversity ▪ Getting Around ▪ Education,
Arts, and Recreation

Chapter Four   73
Government: Law of the Land
Inside Government ▪ Voters, the Law, and the Courts ▪ Whose State Is This? ▪
Land-Use Issues

Chapter Five   87
Economy: Making a Living
Changing with the Times ▪ Working on Land and Sea ▪ The Cost of Living

Chapter Six   99
Landmarks: By Land, Sea, and Air
Up the Inside Passage ▪ South Central and Anchorage ▪ The Southwest ▪
North to the Future ▪ The Heart of Alaska

State Survey   115

Find Out More   139

Index   141

Alaska Is . . .

Alaska is the biggest state in the United States and one of the most challenging places in the country to live.

"Alaska should have been a nation. It's too majestic, too massive to be a mere state."

    —Walter "Wally" Hickel, twice governor of Alaska

"There is risk in getting around in this country, and you can't let fear of flying (or boats or even wild animals) keep you from it—or you might as well live in New York."

    —Heather Lende, journalist who wrote *If You Lived Here,
I'd Know Your Name* about life in Haines

Alaska is both glorious and harsh.

"To the lover of pure wilderness Alaska is one of the most wonderful countries in the world."

    —naturalist John Muir, *Travels in Alaska* (1915)

"This country'll kill you if you're stupid. Or just unlucky."

    —park ranger, Gates of the Arctic National Park and Preserve

Its Native people struggle to balance the old and the new . . .

"Shishmaref is where it is because of what the ocean, rivers, streams and the land provide to us. We are hunters, and we are gatherers. We have been here for countless generations. We value our way of life. It provides for our very existence."

    —Luci Eningowuk, Native resident of Shishmaref,
a village threatened by global warming

"I liked the life we used to live a long time ago, but we were always in need of something. I would say we live in comfort now. I don't go in hunger now. I say both lives I led were good, and I like both."
  —Mary Ann Sundown, a Yupik Native from the Bering Sea coastline

. . . while all Alaskans hope to preserve the unique joys and freedoms of life in "the last frontier."

"[Wrangell–Saint Elias National Park] houses some of our greatest national treasures—free-thinking, cantankerous Alaskans."
  —reporter Nancy Shute

"Our former governor Jay Hammond used to note: Alaska's not just a great state; it's a state of mind. We all need our dreams, and Alaska provides the fuel to keep them going."
  —Bill Perhach, bus driver in Denali National Park

"What's more fun than coming to the end of the road?"
  —Ohio-born Rebecca Bard, who settled in the tiny Alaskan town of McCarthy

Sprawling across the northwestern corner of North America, Alaska was probably the first home of the Native Americans. Today it is home to many different peoples, though the Native presence remains strong. Alaska has always been a land of extremes—the farthest, biggest, coldest, and wildest place. Like all frontiers, it has attracted its share of adventurers and dreamers, loners and misfits, giving rise to the image of a place where everyone is a rugged individualist. Now Alaska's people face the challenge of working together to steer their state into a future of social, economic, and environmental change.

Chapter One

The Great Land

Alaskans don't know for certain how their state got its name. Everyone agrees that the name comes from a Native American word, but people have different ideas about which word it is. Some think that it comes from a language of the Native Inupiaq people. Their word *alaxsxaq*, which means "that which receives the force of the sea," has been suggested as the source of the state name. Most people, though, believe that Alaska was originally called Alyeska. In the language of the Aleut, another of Alaska's Native peoples, *alyeska* means "the great land."

Each word makes sense as a source for Alaska's name. As far as the sea is concerned, Alaska feels its force on three sides, where the North Pacific and Arctic oceans surge against its shores. Those shores are long—counting all of its islands and peninsulas, Alaska has a coastline that is longer than all the coastlines of the rest of the United States added together. And is Alaska a great land? Just ask the more than a million visitors who come to the state every year to marvel at its natural beauty. Many of them would agree with

Alaska's landscape is a varied one of coastal forests, arctic tundra, mountains, and glaciers.

Richard Ulmer of Florida, who declared, "On a scale of one to ten, I rate Alaska as a twenty."

Yet no place is perfect, not even Alaska. The state's inhabitants, Natives and newcomers alike, must deal with a climate that can be brutal and unforgiving. They must answer urgent questions about how to balance economic development with environmental protection. And while most Alaskans realize that mass tourism is vital to their state's future, some fear losing the qualities that make their home unique. In Alaska, the Last Frontier, life can be beautiful, but it is rarely easy.

THE BIGGEST STATE

The single most important fact about Alaska, the thing that astounds every visitor and shapes the life of every resident, is the size of the place. Alaska is one-fifth the size of the rest of the United States. Texans are proud of how big their state is—but Alaska is two and a half times as large.

Alaska is not just big, it's also filled with big things. It has the highest mountain in North America: Denali, formerly called Mount McKinley, which is 20,320 feet high. It has the country's largest national park, Wrangell–Saint Elias (8,331,604 acres); its largest national forest, Tongass (almost 17 million acres); and its largest state park, Wood-Tikchik (1.6 million acres). Alaska also has the world's longest chain of active volcanoes. It has more glaciers, or moving ice fields, than the rest of the inhabited world, and the biggest ones are larger than the state of Rhode Island. Even Alaska's natural disasters are huge. The most powerful recorded earthquake in North American history rocked south central Alaska in 1964.

The second key fact about Alaska is that, like Hawaii, it is separated from the rest of the United States. Alaska is bordered on the north by the Arctic Ocean and on the south by the Gulf of Alaska and the Pacific Ocean.

To the west are the Bering Sea and the Chukchi Sea, with Russia on the other side. At their closest points, Russia and Alaska are only fifty-one miles apart. To the east is Canada. Alaskans call the rest of the continental United States, below Canada, the Lower or South 48.

Bounded with water on three sides, Alaska has a coastline that is 33,000 miles long.

LAND AND WATER

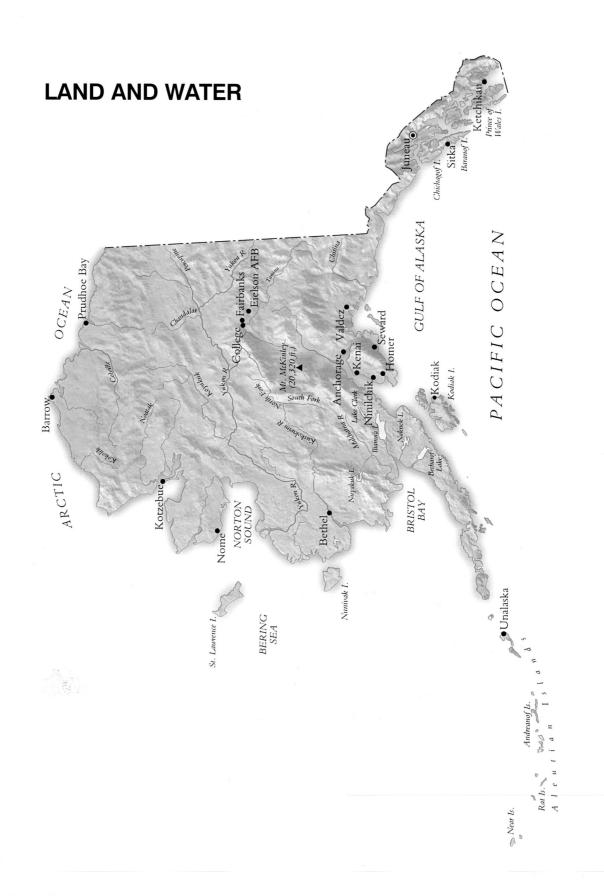

FIVE REGIONS

Alaska is shaped roughly like a square standing on two legs. One leg is the Panhandle, which runs southeast along the coast of Canada. The other is the Alaska Peninsula, which stretches southwest and then breaks up into a 1,600-mile-long chain of islands called the Aleutians—the home of the Aleuts. The state's five geographic regions are the southeast, the south central, the southwest, the interior, and the far north.

Southeast

Alaska's southeastern Panhandle is a region of water and land, a narrow strip of islands, inlets, and peninsulas. The Inside Passage is a waterway that threads among the islands, sheltering ships from the storms of the open northern Pacific Ocean. To the east, the Coast Mountains of British Columbia march along the passage in snowcapped majesty.

Alaska's Inside Passage has one thousand islands and 15,000 miles of coastline, with thousands of coves and bays.

"This place is like a picture from a calendar or something," said the tourist Martine Wirley, watching from the deck of a cruise ship as the morning fog lifted. Ahead, a ribbon of silver water wound between dozens of islands carpeted with dark green spruce and hemlock trees. "It's the most peaceful place I've ever seen."

South Central

At the top of the Panhandle, the U.S. Coast Ranges give way to the rugged Saint Elias Mountains, marking the beginning of south central Alaska, a region of mountains, glaciers, forests, lakes, and streams. This steep and dramatic landscape was shaped by huge ice sheets that carved deep, narrow valleys during ice ages many thousands of years ago.

The Saint Elias, Chugach, and Talkeetna mountains follow the coast. A little inland are the Wrangell Mountains. Still farther inland sweeps the Alaska Range. Many of the mountains are volcanoes, part of the "Ring of Fire" that encircles the Pacific Ocean. These ranges also contain most of the state's 29,000 square miles of glaciers. Some glaciers cling to high mountain slopes, while others flow like sluggish rivers of ice through the valleys. The spectacular tidewater glaciers drop into the sea.

At the middle of the southern coast is the Kenai Peninsula. The Kenai Mountains run the length of the peninsula. On either side are huge, deep inlets of the sea: Prince William Sound on the east and Cook Inlet on the west.

Southwest

Southwestern Alaska begins at the long Alaska Peninsula, with the Aleutian mountain range as its backbone. These mountains seethe and hiss with volcanic life. Mount Pavlof, near the end of the peninsula, has erupted more than forty times since 1762. The biggest recorded eruption in Alaska occurred there in June 1912, when a volcano in what is now Katmai

Worthington Glacier, in the Chugach Mountains, covers an area of almost five square miles.

National Park hurled so much ash into the air that skies were darkened over much of the Northern Hemisphere.

Lake Iliamna in the southwest covers 1,150 square miles and is the largest of the state's 3 million lakes. Kodiak Island, at 3,588 square miles, is the second-largest island in the United States, after Hawaii. Farther west are broad plains, sprinkled with lakes, where the Yukon and Kuskokwim rivers meet the Bering Sea.

The Aleutian Islands trail out to sea like the tail on a kite. These hilly, grass-covered islands are remote and not easy to reach, but they have a rugged beauty all their own. Abi Woodbridge owns a gift shop in Unalaska, the largest city in the islands. "There's something magical about this place," Woodbridge said. "When I came here in 1974, I just knew I was home."

Interior

The interior of Alaska is bordered on the south by the towering Alaska Range, where Denali rises. Beyond the Alaska Range are the Kuskokwim, Kaiyuh, Ray, and White mountains. These ranges are low and weathered, giving the land a broad, rolling appearance.

Denali, formerly known as Mount McKinley, was called the "High One" by Athabascan Native peoples. At its highest, Denali reaches 20,320 feet.

More than half the length of the Yukon River is within Alaska; the rest flows through Canada's Yukon Territory.

The Yukon River, which winds lazily between the ranges, is the chief geographic feature of this part of Alaska. The Yukon is the third-longest river in the United States, after the Mississippi and the Missouri. It flows all the way across the Alaskan interior, from the Canadian border to the Yukon Delta. Its course cuts through a low-lying region called the Yukon Flats, covered with moist, boggy terrain called muskeg and infested with mosquitoes.

Far North

Alaska's far north begins with the Seward Peninsula and the Brooks Range. The Seward Peninsula is a broad, mostly treeless arm of land reaching toward Russia. The Brooks Range is a series of mountain ranges that separate Alaska's interior from the North Slope, a broad plain that runs down to the Arctic Ocean. Part of the peninsula and all of the North Slope are tundra, a generally flat landscape covered with tough mosses and hardy grasses. The only trees that grow in the tundra look more like low shrubs. Willow trees are only a few inches tall.

Several feet beneath the ground's surface is permafrost, frozen soil that never thaws and cannot absorb water. During the brief northern summer, surface water forms a web of lakes and ponds across the tundra, which blazes with the brilliant colors of short-lived wildflowers.

The Brooks Range, located on the edge of Alaska's North Slope region, is the most northern section of the Rocky Mountains.

During summer and early autumn, the tundra becomes ablaze with color.

People who live there build their houses on posts. Otherwise, the warmth from the houses would melt the permafrost, turning the tundra to mud, and the houses would sink. Even with the posts, the ground under a tundra house can get soggy. Some families have to move their houses every few years.

RAIN, SNOW, AND WIND

"Alaska's almost big enough to be a continent in itself," said a weather reporter in Anchorage, in the south central region. "We have half a dozen different climates. The south coast is as different from the north coast as Texas is from Minnesota."

Southern Alaska has a maritime climate, meaning that the sea keeps temperatures from becoming extremely hot or cold. The far north is the coldest region all year round. The interior of Alaska sees the most extreme temperature changes. The lowest *and* highest temperatures ever recorded in Alaska came from the interior: −80 degrees Fahrenheit at Prospect Creek Camp in 1971 and 100°F at Fort Yukon in 1915. The people of Fairbanks, the biggest city of the interior, have learned to make the best of their harsh weather. Every March they hold an Ice Art Championship. All around the town, artists carve huge chunks of ice into dragons, mermaids, and other shapes.

"To tell you about how cold it can get in Alaska," recalled Jerry Jacka, who used to live in Fairbanks, "one day I bought groceries and accidentally left the bananas in the car. That night the temperature dropped to thirty degrees below zero. The next morning the bananas were hard as rocks, and when I tapped them together they sounded like some sort of musical instrument. I made banana bread out of them and have had a beautiful singing voice ever since. Well, that last line is a little bit of an exaggeration, but most stories from Alaska are."

The Panhandle gets a lot of rain but little snow except in the mountains. In contrast, snow blankets much of the interior during winter. The North Slope receives less, but there the biting wind molds the snow into deep drifts. High winds are an Alaskan weather hazard. Alaskans even have special names for their winds. Williwaws are sudden, unexpected gusts. Takus are bitterly cold, fast winds that rush down from ice caps high in the mountains onto southeastern communities. Chinooks are fast, warm winter winds that thaw ice and snow, destroy homes, and knock down power lines.

Alaskans survive their state's cold temperatures by wearing insulated clothing and not exposing skin to the elements.

IT'S GETTING WARMER

During the past hundred years, the average annual temperature of the earth has risen about 1 degree Celsius. Scientists call this effect global warming. Not all of them agree on how much such human activities as burning fossil fuels and creating air pollution have contributed to global warming, but nearly all of them agree that it is happening. Whether the heat rise is part of a natural cycle, a human-caused disaster, or both, global warming is having a big effect on Alaska.

Over the past century the state's average annual temperature has risen more than twice as much as that of the whole planet—between 2 and 3°C (3.5 to 5°F). The difference is due to what climate scientists call the feedback effect. As the white snow and ice of the far north melt away, they reveal dark water or land, which absorbs more heat than the white covering had absorbed. The change from light surfaces to dark ones speeds up the warming of the region.

Rising temperatures are causing many changes. Trees in Alaska's forests are under attack by insect pests, such as spruce bark beetles, that used to be limited by the cold. Such nonnative plants as sweet white clover, once confined to a few scarce patches, are now spreading fast because they thrive in the warmer conditions. In some places, clover is threatening to crowd out the native willow and cottonwood that support Alaska's moose population. In Denali National Park open brushland is gradually becoming more forested. The change may drive away the park's caribou and, possibly, the wolves that feed on them.

The cap of sea ice that once blanketed much of the Arctic Ocean has shrunk by 5 to 10 percent over the past century or so, and some scientists claim that it is now shrinking faster than ever. Alaska's glorious glaciers are feeling the heat, too. According to a 2004 article in

Chunks of tidewater glaciers sometimes break off with loud crashes and fall into the sea. This dramatic event is called glacial calving.

National Parks magazine, a survey of a hundred glaciers found that all but three of them have gotten thinner. Many have shrunk in area as well. Scientists estimate that meltwater from glaciers, flowing into the oceans, is responsible for about 10 percent of the total rise in sea level around the world.

Rising sea levels are one problem. Sinking land is another, and melting ice is a third. All three have made life difficult for the residents of Shishmaref, a village of the Native Inupiaq people on the Bering Sea coast. The permafrost under Shishmaref is melting, causing the village to sink. Worse yet, the sea ice that once protected the shore is disappearing, allowing huge waves to erode the land beneath homes and village buildings. The remaining ice is thinner than it used to be, which makes it harder for hunters to venture onto it to hunt bearded seals, a staple of the residents' diet. Every aspect of traditional life, from fishing to hunting to gathering berries, has had to adapt to changes in age-old seasonal patterns. "If the weather keeps changing," said the resident Percy Nayokpuk, "it will be the end of Shishmaref."

Most residents of Shishmaref do not want to drift into Alaska's cities. They desperately want their way of life and their village to remain intact, so they have voted to relocate the entire town to a more protected site a few miles inland. It's not yet clear, though, whether such a move is practical—or who will pay for it. And Shishmaref is not alone. A study by the federal government found that three other villages are in immediate danger of washing away, while twenty others are threatened.

Nayokpuk and many other Alaskans know firsthand that the physical world around them is changing in ways beyond their control. Gunter Weller, the director of the Center for Global Change and

Arctic System Research at the University of Alaska in Fairbanks, said, "In Alaska, people are more aware of the warming problem because it's staring you in the face. You can't deny the evidence, because it's all around you."

DAY AND NIGHT

Alaska is sometimes called the Land of the Midnight Sun. The farther north you go in summertime, the longer the days and the shorter the nights. The Arctic Circle marks the point where the sun doesn't set at all on the longest day of summer. North of the Arctic Circle the sun stays in the sky for days at a time. In Barrow, on the north coast, the sun rises on May 10 and doesn't set until August 2, eighty-four days later. Many northern communities celebrate the midnight sun of summer. The people of Nome, for example, hold a midsummer festival that includes a softball tournament, raft and mountain bike races, a barbecued-chicken feast, and a pie-eating contest.

For every long summer day, however, there will be a long winter night. During the winter northern days get shorter and nights get longer. At the Arctic Circle the sun doesn't rise at all on the shortest day of the year. In Barrow the sun sets on November 18 and doesn't rise until January 24. "Land of the Midnight Sun sounds good," said Anita Rees, who lives in a cabin in the interior, "but Alaska could just as truly be called Land of the Dark Noon."

Some Alaskans suffer from cabin fever, feelings of restlessness or sadness during the long, dark winters, when people spend most of their time indoors. Tempers can wear thin by spring. The former governor Tony Knowles once said, "April is one tough month. Expectations rise as spring approaches, but if it stays cold or snows in April, people find that spring hasn't provided a cure-all. They go crazy." Harold Weaver, a former newspaper editor in Anchorage, said, "Some people can't handle the cold and the dark. They come alive again when they can shake off their cabin fever."

This is a time-lapsed photo showing the sun's rise and dip during the summer solstice, the day that has the most hours of sunshine.

"THIS GLORY OF LIGHT"

The night sky of Alaska often shimmers and glows with the eerily beautiful northern lights, or aurora borealis. In the late 1800s the naturalist John Muir visited Alaska and was carried away by what he called "this glory of light, so pure, so bright, so enthusiastic in motion."

The northern lights can appear as bands of color that stretch across the sky or as sheets of light that ripple like immense silken curtains in the heavens. Some people say that the lights make a rustling or swishing sound, but no one has been able to prove this. Electrical energy from the sun, drawn to the polar regions by the earth's magnetic field, strikes gas particles in the earth's upper atmosphere and causes them to light up.

You don't have to go to Alaska to see the northern lights. The aurora borealis appears across Canada and is sometimes seen in the Lower 48. But Alaskans have a much better chance of viewing it than most Americans. In Fairbanks the northern lights may be watched about 240 nights a year.

WILD ALASKA

Wildlife is one of Alaska's glories. Its coastal waters are home to many kinds of fish, seabirds, sea otters, walruses, seals, sea lions, and whales. Sitka black-tailed deer and moose live in the south. Moose feed on the spruce, aspen, and willow forests of the interior.

Alaska has three kinds of bears: black, brown (also called grizzlies), and polar. Black bears are common in the south and in the interior. Brown bears thrive in nearly all parts of the state. The Kodiak is a type of large brown bear native to Kodiak Island. Polar bears, weighing up to 1,500 pounds when fully grown, live along the northern and northwestern coasts and have been spotted swimming as far as fifty miles from land.

"Alaskans love telling bear stories, and the wilder the better," wrote the backpacker Jim Gorman after a visit to Chugach State Park near Anchorage. Most of the stories are about the brown bear, which one old-time Alaskan hunter called "a mountain of fur and teeth." Although brown bears have attacked and killed people, such attacks are rare. "Bears don't *want* to encounter people," said a wildlife biologist. "If a bear hears you coming, he'll get out of your way."

In wilderness areas the song of the wolf floats through the Alaskan night. Wolves prey on young or sick deer and other large mammals, but most of the time they live on such small creatures as lemmings, mouse-like rodents of the tundra.

Caribou roam the northern tundra in huge herds that may total 200,000 animals. Every winter they cross the Brooks Range to spend the cold months foraging for food in the interior. Musk oxen, shaggy-haired wild cattle, used to live in the far north, but hunters killed the last ones in 1865. Later, people transported musk oxen from Greenland to start new populations in Alaska.

Brown bears thrive in Alaska, feeding on fish, livestock, deer, elk, and berries.

Caribou migrate in order to find enough food for the entire herd.

At least 430 kinds of birds have been sighted in Alaska. Some of them, such as ravens, bald eagles, ptarmigans, and snowy owls, live there all year long. Others spend only the spring and summer months in Alaska, feeding and breeding and raising their young. Uncountable millions of ducks, geese, and waterbirds migrate annually to Alaska's lakes and marshes from all around the world. The Arctic tern makes the longest journey of any bird: a 22,000-mile round-trip each year between Alaska and Antarctica.

Two of Alaska's bird species—the short-tailed albatross and the Eskimo curlew—are on the U.S. government's list of endangered species. Alaska's other endangered species are the Aleutian shield fern (the state's only plant on the list), the leatherback sea turtle, the eastern population of Steller sea lions, and three species of whales: bowhead, finback, and humpback. The northern sea otter and the western population of Steller

Humpback whales are usually found near the southern coast of Alaska. Researchers believe they breach (above) during courtship or as play.

sea lions are considered threatened, a condition that is less severe than being endangered but still cause for concern about the species' long-term survival. Also threatened are two species of ducklike birds, the Steller's eider and the spectacled eider.

One bird nearly became extinct but has made a comeback in Alaska and elsewhere—the Arctic peregrine falcon. This bird hovered on the brink of extinction in the 1970s because of such chemicals as the pesticide DDT. The falcons, who hunt mice and other small creatures, ate the pesticides along with their prey. These chemicals caused severe problems for the falcons and for other birds as well. One of the worst effects was that birds poisoned by DDT laid eggs with thin, defective shells, so that they were unable to raise young successfully.

Two things saved the Arctic peregrine falcon. First, the United States and some other countries banned DDT. Second, wildlife biologists in Alaska and other parts of the falcon's northern range bred falcons in

Peregrine *also means "wanderer." This falcon can migrate over 15,000 miles in one year.*

captivity, taught them to hunt, prepared them for life in the wild, and then released them in their natural habitat. These new falcon populations grew over time. In fact, by 1994 the Arctic peregrine falcon was removed from the endangered species list. Today the falcons once again nest and rear their young on Alaska's tundra, then fly thousands of miles to spend the winter in South America before returning for another nesting season in the north.

The grizzly bear is majestic and the wolf is wily, but Alaska's most feared wild creature may just be the mosquito. Enormous swarms of mosquitoes hatch in pools all over the state every summer. Stinging and humming, thick clouds of these insects have been known to drive caribou into rivers and people into hysterics.

WHERE THE PEOPLE ARE

People and the things they build are part of the Alaskan landscape. With an area of 656,425 square miles and a population estimated at 640,000 in 2005, Alaska has 0.91 people for every square mile in the state. Compare this with 79 people per square mile in the United States as a whole, or more than 26,000 per square mile in New York City, and you'll see that Alaska is very thinly populated.

There are many thousands of square miles where nobody lives. In building cities and roads and in carrying out such economic activities as farming, mining, and logging, people have directly affected less than 1 percent of the land in the state. The greatest concentration of people—and of their cities, villages, and roads—is along the southern coast. More than half of all Alaskans live in or near Anchorage. On the other hand, there are numerous tiny communities like Red Devil, a town on the Kuskokwim River that has forty-eight inhabitants.

Chapter Two

The Making of Alaska

The first people in the Americas came from Asia, and the first place they set foot was probably Alaska. They crossed the Bering Sea on a land bridge that emerged during the ice ages, when much of the earth's water was frozen in huge glaciers and its seas were shallower.

Scientists are seeking answers to many questions about the arrival of humans in the Americas. All agree that bands of hunters crossed from Siberia to North America and that a human population was established in the Americas by about 12,000 years ago. Some researchers, though, think that the migrations may have begun thousands of years earlier. At any rate, these wanderers gradually spread outward to become the ancestors of all the original peoples of North and South America. Around 12,000 years ago the ice melted and the waters rose, covering the land bridge. By that time, however, the people of the far north could cross the Bering Strait by boat.

THE FIRST ALASKANS

The Native people of Alaska formed many different cultures. These cultures fell into four main groups: the Indians, the Aleuts, the Yupik, and the

This watercolor by Theodore J. Richardson shows a Tlingit village at Wrangell.

Inupiaq (the Yupik and Inupiaq are referred to as Eskimos in the United States, and in Canada the Inupiaq are known as the Inuit). When Europeans first encountered the Alaskans in the mid-1700s, each group lived in a separate region. All lived by hunting, fishing, and gathering such wild foods as berries and roots.

The Indians

The Tlingit, Haida, and Tshimshian Indians lived in the southeast. They had moved there from what is now Canada and were closely related to other Native peoples along the coast of British Columbia. The Tlingit were traders, and the Haida were noted for making fine tools and art objects from wood, stone, bone, and shell. All three groups were skilled woodworkers who made dugout canoes and carved cedar totem poles that served as records of their legends and histories.

The Athabascan Indians roamed Alaska's vast interior, scratching a living from the harsh land and sometimes battling famine or starvation. They consisted of many tribes. Each had its own dialect, but they were culturally related to each other and to such other varied Native American groups as the Navajo and the Apache in the American Southwest. The Athabascans did not build permanent settlements, but traveled from place to place, following such game as caribou and moose. They used snowshoes to walk while hunting during the winter. Some Athabascans lived on the coast around Cook Inlet and relied on salmon as a major part of their diet.

H. W. Elliot produced this engraving of Alaskan Natives trading for oil.

Athabascans produced fine garments made of skins, often decorated with fringe or beads. They traded with other coastal Indians, exchanging skin clothing and animal furs for such items as fish and carved wooden objects.

The Aleuts

The smallest Native group in Alaska was the Aleut, whose members occupied the end of the Alaska Peninsula and the Aleutian Islands. The Aleuts lived in large houses in permanent villages, with as many as forty families sharing one house. They were the foremost mariners among the Native peoples. In sturdy skin-covered canoes called *baidarkas*, they skillfully navigated the dangerous, foggy seas around their islands, sometimes making voyages of several hundred miles. Aleut women used needles made from the bones of seagulls to decorate their clothing with fine embroidery.

Aleut fishermen hunted for small whales in skin-covered canoes.

The Yupik and Inupiaq

The peoples who are referred to as Eskimos settled all across the northern coastline of North America, from the Bering Sea across Canada to Greenland. Two different populations occupied Alaska. The Inupiaq occupied the north coast, while the Yupik lived on Kodiak Island, the upper Alaska Peninsula, and the west coast, along the Bering Sea.

Scientists think that these were probably the last Native groups to cross over from Asia, and they were closely related to peoples on the Siberian coast. They lived in houses called *barabaras*, which were made of thick pieces of sod (slabs of grassy earth) on a framework of driftwood or whale bones. They gathered berries, hunted moose and caribou, and fished for salmon, but sea mammals—whales, seals, and walruses—were their major sources of food,

In Seal Hunters, *Belmore Brown depicts Alaskan Natives hunting seal in a traditional canoe.*

skins, and oil for lamps. Today some Yupik and Inupiaq still hunt as their ancestors did. Every June, for example, the Inupiaq celebrate their hunting traditions at the Nalukataq Whaling Festival at Barrow, on the north coast.

RUSSIAN ALASKA

In the 1500s Russians in Europe looked eastward and began exploring and colonizing Siberia. Slowly they moved toward Asia's Pacific coast. Czar Peter the Great sent Vitus Bering, a Danish officer serving in the Russian navy, to see if Siberia and North America were joined by land. In 1728 Bering sailed north through the fifty-three-mile-wide strait that now bears his name, proving that Asia and the Americas are not connected. But he didn't see America, which was hidden by fog. In 1741 he tried again to locate the northwestern coast of America, and this time he succeeded.

Bering's men were the first Europeans to cross the sea that bears his name. They went ashore on Kayak Island, off Alaska's south coast. There Georg Steller, a German naturalist who sailed with Bering, found what he called "signs of people and their doings," such as cut trees and bones, dried salmon, and ropes made of seaweed.

Bering's men carried sea otter skins back to Russia, where the soft, silky furs caused a sensation. Soon Russian traders and adventurers were heading to the Aleutian Islands for furs, which fetched high prices in Europe and China. By the end of the 1700s, the sea otter was almost extinct. Tragically, the Russians nearly wiped out the Aleuts as well. The Europeans introduced such deadly diseases as smallpox and tuberculosis. They also enslaved the Aleuts and treated them brutally. In 1762, when the Aleuts rebelled against this treatment, the Russians killed thousands of them.

THE GREAT RAVEN BRINGS LIFE

Ravens are clever, shiny black birds, much like crows but larger. They live nearly everywhere in Alaska. According to the Natives of Alaska, all animals and birds have spirits. The raven spirit is especially important in the religion of many Native peoples. Raven has many faces. Sometimes he is a generous giver of gifts, and sometimes he is a trickster or prankster.

The Bering Sea Natives tell many stories about the Great Raven, who created the world. Life began when Raven dropped peas onto the ground. Each pea turned into a man. Raven then made animals out of clay: two bears, two wolves, two squirrels, and so on until he had created all the animals. Finally he took more clay and made a woman, the wife of the first man. That is how animals and people came into the world.

The Russians built their first permanent base in Alaska in 1784 at Three Saints Bay, on Kodiak Island. Under their influence, many Natives there learned to speak Russian and adopted the Eastern Orthodox religion, a form of Christianity. The Russian influence lingers on in Kodiak to this day. As they celebrate the Russian New Year and Christmas in early January, islanders follow the Eastern Orthodox tradition of "starring." Led by someone twirling a large star, a choir visits church members' homes to sing hymns. Russian food is served at a big New Year's dinner in the church, after which everyone puts on masks for a costume ball.

In 1799 Czar Paul I put a fur-trading firm called the Russian-American Company in charge of all Russian operations in Alaska. The company sent

Aleksandr Baranov, a merchant from Siberia, to manage the colony. Baranov made his headquarters at Kodiak, but later moved to New Anchorage, near the present-day site of Sitka, in the southeast. The local Tlingit fiercely resisted the Russian invasion, but by 1804 Baranov and his men, along with their Aleut slaves, had seized control of the area.

The American writer Washington Irving called Baranov "a rough, rugged, hospitable, hard-drinking, old Russian, somewhat of a soldier, somewhat of a trader." Under Baranov's leadership, the fur trade prospered, and New Anchorage flourished.

When Aleksandr Baranov took charge of the Russian-American Company in Alaska, the company made him "governor" of the region.

Aleksandr Baranov established a thriving fur-trading organization in Sitka for the Russian-American Company. In 1867 the company folded when Alaska was sold to the United States.

After Baranov retired in 1818, New Anchorage continued to grow. Although tales of New Anchorage being the glamorous "Paris of the North" are exaggerated, the city had a school, library, hospital, and cathedral.

THE UNITED STATES TAKES OVER

By 1867 Russia was busy with European affairs and was losing control of its American colony. The British and the Americans were poised to move in. To keep the British out, Russia offered to sell Alaska to the United States. Secretary of state William Seward wanted his country to acquire this huge territory and its resources of minerals, timber, and fish. He arranged for the United States to buy Alaska for $7.2 million, or two cents an acre.

Seward knew that he had made one of the greatest real estate bargains in history. "But," he said, "it will take the people a generation to find out." Many Americans criticized the purchase, calling Alaska "Seward's Folly." They thought the place was an icy wasteland and couldn't imagine why anyone would want it. They soon found out.

In 1880 two prospectors named Joe Juneau and Richard Harris discovered gold in southeastern Alaska. Within a short time, hundreds of gold hunters had flocked to the site. They founded the town of Juneau, which later became Alaska's capital. A much larger gold rush started in 1896, when prospectors found gold in the Klondike River in Canada's Yukon

William Seward stated that the most important act in his career as a politician was the purchase of Alaska.

Territory. Southern Alaska was the gateway to the Klondike, and by the following year thousands of hopeful gold seekers from all over the world thronged the muddy streets of the tiny town of Skagway, each waiting for his turn to clamber up the steep, dangerous Chilkoot Pass into the Yukon.

In 1898 people found gold on the beaches of Nome, kicking off the biggest and wildest gold rush in American history. By the summer of 1900, more than 230 ships had taken some 18,000 prospectors to western Alaska. Tents sprang up everywhere. Gold seekers who didn't have tents slept on the sand. In the scramble for riches, some resorted to theft and even murder. People still travel to Nome every summer to camp on the beaches and search for gold—but their camps are a lot less rowdy than those of the old-time prospectors!

Gold seekers make their way to the Klondike goldfields through the steep Chilkoot Pass in 1897.

THE KLONDIKE GOLD RUSH

Gold was discovered in Forty Mile Creek in the Yukon Territory in 1887. After a bigger gold strike over the border on the Canadian side in the Klondike River in 1896, people used the term Klondike to refer to both the Alaskan and Canadian diggings. The gold rush to the rugged, frozen north rivaled anything that had been experienced in the Lower 48.

The lawless gold rushes made some Americans think that Alaska needed a dose of law and order. The missionary Sheldon Jackson agreed and became a leader in the movement to bring effective government to Alaska. The preacher Samuel Hall Young came to Alaska to work with Jackson. Young also criticized the federal government for neglecting Alaska. He wrote, "The struggle of Alaskans for their rights as American citizens forms one of the gloomy pages of American history."

The army, the customs office, and the navy had each tried to govern Alaska since 1867, with little success. In 1884 the U.S. Congress named it a district of the United States and tried to establish order by extending Oregon's laws northward. In 1912 Alaska was made a territory, with an elected legislature, or lawmaking body. Alaskans had been allowed to send a representative to Congress since 1906, but that lone delegate still had no vote.

WAR AND STATEHOOD

In 1914 the federal government began building a railroad to connect the harbors of Alaska's south coast with the mines and coalfields of the interior. By then, most gold and copper mining in Alaska was done by large companies that could afford the equipment for underground operations. The salmon-fishing industry was well established along the south coast, with dozens of canneries preparing fish for shipment to other parts of the world. Lumber companies were beginning to harvest the mighty, ancient forests of southern Alaska—the first wood-pulp mill opened near Juneau in 1922. The Great Depression, which plunged much of the world into economic chaos in the 1930s, had little effect on Alaska because gold continued to sell at a high price.

For years, most people in the Lower 48 rarely thought about Alaska. In 1941, however, Japan bombed Pearl Harbor, a U.S. naval base in Hawaii, and the United States declared war on Japan. Americans suddenly realized that part of their nation—the western islands of Alaska—was closer to Japan than to Washington, D.C. Japanese bombers attacked Dutch Harbor, a naval base in the Aleutian Islands, in 1942, and Japanese troops seized the islands of Attu and Kiska. The United States acted quickly, sending about 200,000 soldiers to Alaska. After fighting the Aleutian Campaign, called the Thousand-Mile War, the Americans recaptured Attu and Kiska in 1943.

Six months after the attack on Pearl Harbor, the Japanese attacked Dutch Harbor on June 3, 1942.

When the war began, Alaska could be reached only by ship or airplane. The U.S. government needed a land route to deliver supplies and equipment to support the war effort, and in 1942, with permission from Canada, it created one. In just eight months, in one of the greatest engineering feats of modern times, the Army Corps of Engineers built the first road linking Alaska with the Lower 48 states. It runs for 1,520 miles from Dawson Creek in British Columbia through the Yukon Territory to Fairbanks. Sometimes called the Alcan Highway, the Alaska Highway is still the only road into Alaska.

World War II changed Alaska in several ways. It gave the territory a highway, and thousands of new residents—people who went to Alaska on military service or as workers on military construction sites and then settled there. For a long time Alaskans had been asking Congress to make their enormous territory into a state. Now, with the surge in population, demands for statehood grew louder.

Alaskans believed they could demonstrate that they were ready for statehood by preparing a state constitution. In 1955 they chose delegates from all over the territory to draw one up. The delegates created a document that the National Municipal League called "one of the best, if not the best, state constitutions ever written." Alaska's voters approved the constitution in 1956, and the U.S. Congress passed the Alaska Statehood Act in 1958. Alaska became the forty-ninth state in the Union on January 3, 1959.

For several decades after World War II, high tensions existed between the United States and the communist Soviet Union, which consisted of Russia and several neighboring nations. During this "cold war," Americans feared a Soviet attack. The federal government built radar bases in Alaska as part of a northern network of stations designed to detect any attack and to sound

Delegates William Egan (right) and Bob Bartlett celebrate Alaska's statehood.

the warning. An attack never came, and today most of those stations have been taken out of service or converted to other uses.

The military now has three main responsibilities in Alaska. One is protecting the Trans-Alaska Pipeline in case of attack. Another is contributing to defense, both with troops, who can be sent anywhere in the world they are needed, and with missile sites in Kodiak and other locations. The third function, performed by the Coast Guard, involves law enforcement and search-and-rescue operations in Alaskan waters.

THE RUSH FOR LIQUID GOLD

Soon the new state felt the impact of a different kind of gold rush—a rush for petroleum, or "liquid gold." Pumps in the Kenai Peninsula had been bringing up oil since 1957. Then in 1968 geologists discovered a larger reserve at Prudhoe Bay, on the North Slope. There was just one big problem with this discovery: how would the oil get from the Arctic to world markets?

Petroleum companies wanted to build a pipeline to carry oil and natural gas through Alaska to a port on the south coast. Environmentalists protested. If the pipeline sprang a leak, the spill could harm the wilderness and wildlife. Native peoples whose traditional lands lay along the pipelines route also protested. After the passage of the Alaska Native Claims Settlement Act in 1971, the federal government allowed a group of oil companies to build the Trans-Alaska Pipeline System. The pipeline, completed in 1977, runs for eight hundred miles, from Prudhoe Bay to the ice-free port of Valdez, across eight hundred rivers and streams and through three mountain ranges.

The accident that environmentalists feared didn't come from the pipeline. It came in March 1989, when the oil tanker *Exxon Valdez* ran onto a reef of rock in Prince William Sound and spilled 11 million gallons of oil into what were once crystal-clear waters. The spill was one of the worst ecological disasters the world had ever seen. Wind and tides smeared

One of the largest pipelines in the world, the Trans-Alaska Pipeline has moved more than 14 billion barrels of oil.

hundreds of miles of coastline with sticky oil. More than 200,000 seabirds, 2,800 otters, 300 harbor seals, and 250 eagles perished, soaked with oil. Commercial fisheries in the area were devastated; some remain closed today. A federal jury found the Exxon Corporation and the captain of the *Valdez* guilty of recklessness, and Exxon was ordered to pay billions of dollars for the damage caused by the spill.

Some people believe that the 1989 spill caused less harm than was first feared. "No one wants to know what the truth is. No one wants to know the science behind it," said Jeff Wheelwright, author of *Degrees of Disaster* (1996), who thinks that Prince William Sound has recovered. Some scientists, nonetheless, fear that the long-term effects of the spill won't be known for many years.

Other effects of the oil boom on Alaska are easier to see. Throughout the 1970s and early 1980s people flocked to Alaska to work on the pipeline and in the petroleum industry. The state's population increased by almost one-third during the 1970s. The oil boom boosted incomes and gave the state money for new roads, schools, airstrips, and other construction projects in many areas. Then world oil prices dropped in 1985, and Alaska's oil production and income dropped, too. Oil and natural gas are still very important to the economy, but the "gold rush" days are over.

After the Exxon Valdez *oil spill in 1989, environmentalists worked diligently to clean the oil-covered rocks and wildlife.*

POPULATION GROWTH: 1880–2000

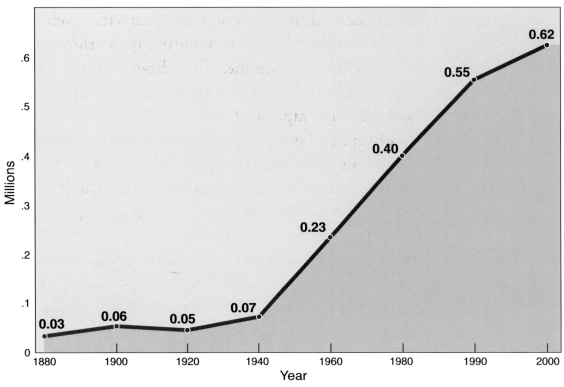

INTO THE TWENTY-FIRST CENTURY

In 1988, as the cold war was drawing to a close, the government of the
Soviet Union, as Russia was then called, allowed a group of Alaskans to
make a one-day visit to the port town of Provideniya in Siberia—the
Russian town closest to Alaska. That visit was noteworthy because the
Soviet government had kept its borders tightly closed for many years,
so the trip paved the way for travel between the two continents. After
the fall of the Soviet government in 1991, regular air service between
Alaska and Siberia became a reality. A few Alaskans have proposed

making travel even easier by either building a bridge across the Bering Strait or digging a tunnel beneath it. Without waiting for such monumental measures, Russians have taken the opportunity to shop in Alaskan stores and attend Alaskan universities. Some have even become permanent residents.

For decades, Alaskans have argued about whether or not they should move their state's capital. Juneau, the capital, is located on Alaska's southeast coast and can be reached only by boat or plane. But although some Alaskans feel that the capital should be located closer to Anchorage, the state's biggest city, voters in 2002 defeated the most recent attempt to move the legislature away from Juneau.

Another Alaskan event of 2002 was felt as far away as Louisiana. On November 3, a 7.9-magnitude earthquake rocked the interior of Alaska. The U.S. Geological Survey ranked the quake among the nine strongest ever to hit the United States. Centered ninety miles south of Fairbanks, the quake caused about $25 million worth of damage to roads and bridges. There were no serious injuries, however, because that part of Alaska is so sparsely populated.

Alaska remained in an economic slump throughout the late 1980s and the 1990s. The state suffered budget problems. Many people lost their jobs and even their homes. A great number of people left the state—the city of Anchorage alone lost 30,000 residents in 1988. Several mines and wood-pulp mills went out of business, putting more Alaskans out of work. By 2004, though, the economy had begun to improve. With a worldwide rise in oil prices, petroleum companies were making increased profits by selling oil from Alaskan wells. The state began considering whether to boost state income by raising the tax it charges these companies for each gallon of oil taken from the ground.

Chapter Three
Life in the Big Beyond

"The first few years I lived here I thought of Alaska as 'the Big Beyond,'" said sixty-eight-year-old Edna Laurie, who grew up in Iowa but has lived in Alaska since she was twenty-four. "When my husband said he wanted to move up here, I couldn't believe my ears. It seemed like moving to the moon. But now it's home."

In his 1976 book *Coming into the Country*, a look at life in the biggest state, John McPhee wrote, "The central paradox of Alaska is that it is as small as it is large—an immense landscape with so few people in it that language is stretched to call it a frontier, let alone a state." Alaska will probably never be crowded. In the past, events that created new jobs and economic activities led to surges in Alaska's population. During and immediately after World War II, for example, the state's population rose sharply. It rose again in the mid-1970s, when the Trans-Alaska Pipeline was built, and in the early 1980s, when income from oil was high. After some population loss in the late 1980s, growth resumed. Between 1990 and 2000 Alaska's population increased by 14 percent (compared to a 13 percent increase for the nation as a whole).

"I love the people here . . . everywhere in Alaska that I've lived or traveled, I've met extraordinary people." — Artist Elise Tomlinson

NATIVE ALASKA

Alaska has a higher proportion of Native Americans in its population than any other state. Almost 16 percent of Alaskans are Natives. About half of them are Yupik or Inupiaq. One-third of Alaska's Natives live in Anchorage or Fairbanks. The rest live in smaller communities scattered along the coast and rivers. In western and northern Alaska and in parts of the interior, the majority of the population is Native.

Life changed forever for these peoples when the Europeans came. Mary Ann Sundown lived through the years of change. She was born into a traditional Yupik community near Scammon Bay, on the Bering Sea coast. Mary Ann grew up in a sod house with a single window made of dried seal gut and a lamp that burned seal oil for light. She didn't see a white person until she was fifteen years old. Today her grandchildren ride snowmobiles and read fashion magazines.

Native Alaskans account for almost 16 percent of the state's total population.

Fred Ewan of the Ahtna, an Athabascan group in southeastern Alaska, also remembers the old ways. "We ate moose, caribou, sheep, ducks, and swans. Also berries, the roots of wild rhubarb, and wild onion. We caught salmon in fish traps made from spruce branches the size of your thumb. Now," he said, "the young people eat white man's food."

Alaska's Natives lost many ties to their old ways during the 1800s and the first half of the 1900s. Missionaries and government officials tried to stamp out their languages, customs, and beliefs because they thought that the best thing for the Natives was to make them as much like white people as possible. Yet Natives were not fully accepted as equals in white society. As a result, many of them felt that they lived in two worlds but didn't truly belong in either. Many of these Natives struggled with alcoholism and depression.

"Many of us are unskilled, uneducated, and lost in the predominant [white] culture," Roy Huhndorf, head of the Cook Inlet Region Native Corporation, said in 1988. "Alaska Natives exist in a time warp, and we've been victimized by it. Why do you suppose that we have such a high degree of alcoholism, drug addiction, suicide? I think cultural dislocation is the culprit." Huhndorf added, "We've lost our culture. . . . Our old ways are going, going, gone."

Yet things have begun to get better since the Alaska Native Claims Settlement Act of 1971, which restored to Native Alaskans some of the land and resources they had lost. The Native corporations created by the act have invested the money the act awarded to Natives. These corporations now own and operate many businesses, from sawmills to hotels to computer-manufacturing companies. Natives are also taking a growing part in state and local governments. To deal with alcohol abuse, some Native communities have outlawed alcohol.

Moreover, young Natives are once again learning the traditions, arts, customs, and languages of their ancestors. Mary Ann Sundown's grandchildren learn the Yupik language in school, get together with friends to perform traditional Yupik dances, and learn traditional hunting methods from their father. Her daughter said, "I want them to learn other ways—outside ways. And I want them to learn our way, too, hunting for our kind of foods. We can't have store-bought food all the time. I want them to learn both ways."

Native Alaskan heritage and culture are passed down from generation to generation. Here, a child is wearing a Tlingit mask.

The pull of the outside world is strong for many young Natives, and most elders realize that it would not be possible to return completely to their old ways. But some people are trying to build a way of life that combines the best of the old and the new. Paul Ongtooguk, an Inupiaq, teaches Native studies in Kotzebue. He hopes that the meeting of Native and white cultures can benefit both. "Here, in Alaska," he said, "we're trying to be optimistic that the three-hundred-year legacy of conflict between Western society and Native America will somehow turn out different. Alaskan Natives have the opportunity to become another downtrodden minority, or we have an opportunity to create a very successful synthesis [union] between our own society and Western society."

With growing pride in their heritage, Alaska's Natives have revived festivals and customs that were almost lost. In 1988, two thousand Inupiaq of the north coast gathered in Barrow for a *kivgiq*, or messenger feast, a celebration that had not been held for seventy years. A kivgiq was an occasion for villages and individuals to exchange gifts. At the 1988 festival, gifts included a polar bear skin given by a coastal community to a village in the Brooks Range and a pair of walrus tusks given by a hunter to a skilled carver. Feasts of traditional foods such as whale meat were alternated with storytelling and drumming. Dancers imitating the movements of birds and animals competed in contests.

The kivgiq was such a success that it is now held every year. A community leader explained, "There is a social and spiritual need inside us as Inupiaq which can only be satisfied by our own traditions." An ancient tradition has been restored—except that instead of sending a messenger from village to village to spread word of the feast, today's Inupiaq use fax machines and e-mail.

ETHNIC ALASKA

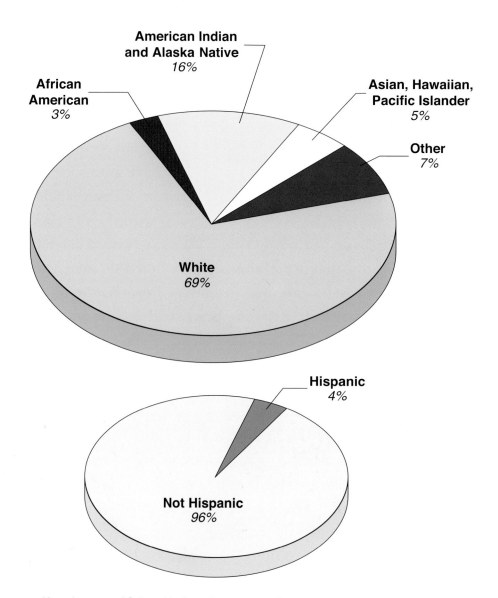

**American Indian
and Alaska Native**
16%

**African
American**
3%

**Asian, Hawaiian,
Pacific Islander**
5%

Other
7%

White
69%

Hispanic
4%

Not Hispanic
96%

*Note: A person of Cuban, Mexican, Puerto Rican, South or Central American,
or other Spanish culture or origin, regardless of race, is defined as Hispanic.*

ETHNIC AND CULTURAL DIVERSITY

Although Alaska is becoming more and more ethnically diverse, with growing populations of Asian, Hispanic, and South Pacific people, about 69 percent of Alaskans are white. Among these, more than 16 percent claim German ancestry, almost 10 percent are of English descent, and about 4 percent have Norwegian roots. The largest minority in the state is Native, at 15.6 percent of the total population. The next largest minority is the Hispanic community, which makes up 4.1 percent of the total.

While over 65 percent of the population is white, Alaska's ethnic diversity is growing.

Another 4 percent of Alaskans are ethnically Asian, while 3.5 percent are black. Larger than the Hispanic, Asian, and African-American groups, however, is the mixed-race population of Alaska, 5.4 of the state's total population. In Alaska, as elsewhere in the country, the mixed-race population has grown rapidly for two reasons. First, social changes are breaking down the barriers to intermarriage. Second, census takers and other record keepers today make greater efforts to recognize mixed-race and multiracial identities.

Language and religion reflect the ethnic and cultural patterns of Alaska's past and present. About 85.7 percent of Alaskans over the age of five speak English as their primary language. Another 5.2 percent speak a Native language as their primary language. English is dominant because for years Natives were discouraged from using their traditional languages and were required to speak English. Now they can choose to speak Native languages, but many have forgotten them or never learned them in the first place. Many other languages are spoken in Alaska as well. Fewer than 3 percent of Alaskans speak primarily Spanish, 1.5 speak Tagalog (a language from the Philippines), and 0.8 speak Korean. Anchorage's schools teach children speaking more than seventy languages!

Where religion is concerned, Alaska is overwhelmingly Christian. About 81 percent of Alaskans identify themselves with some form of Christianity. Most are Protestant (68 percent), but there are also Catholics (7 percent) and Mormons (1 percent). As a lingering result of Alaska's Russian heritage, 8 percent of Alaskans belong to the Eastern Orthodox Church, a greater percentage than in any other state. One percent of Alaskans practice such other religions as Islam or Buddhism, while 17 percent do not consider themselves religious.

For thousands of years, the firm, pink flesh of the salmon has been an important food source for many of Alaska's Natives. But these nutritious fish are not available all year round, so Native Alaskans learned to hang strips of salmon in smoke. Fish dried and smoked this way remain good to eat for many months. You can enjoy this Alaskan treat in a modern way, and you don't even have to catch a fish or build a fire. Just buy a small package of smoked salmon, also called lox. (Most grocery stores carry this traditional food.)

You'll also want:
Crackers or thin slices of bread (pumpernickel bread is good
  with salmon)
Cream cheese or slices of your favorite cheese
A selection of sliced dill pickles, lemon juice, seafood cocktail
  sauce, or capers

Spread the cream cheese on a cracker or piece of bread. Now flake off a chunk of the smoked salmon, using a fork, and put it on top of the cheese. You can eat this delicious treat just as it is, but some people like to top it off with a slice of pickle, a squirt of lemon juice, or a dab of spicy seafood cocktail sauce. Use your imagination to come up with other combinations. Is this a snack or a meal? *That* depends on how much you eat!

GETTING AROUND

Getting around in Alaska can be a challenge. Although the Kenai Peninsula, the port of Valdez, and Fairbanks are linked by a network of highways, there are few other major roads in the state. A single gravel road leads from Fairbanks to Prudhoe Bay. The Alaska Highway is the only paved road leading into or out of the whole state.

Huge portions of Alaska cannot be reached by road at all. Alaskans call these roadless areas the Bush. They make an exception, though, for their capital city. Juneau is not considered part of the Bush even though it can be reached only by sea or air—or on foot.

Anchorage and Fairbanks, and their suburbs, have streets like those in the Lower 48. In most communities, however, none of the streets go very far. A tour operator in Barrow remarked to a magazine reporter, "There are twenty-eight miles of road out here, and all of them dead end."

Alaskans have found ways to get around in the Bush. All-terrain vehicles are popular in summer. When snow covers the ground, some people follow the traditional northern Native practice of using dog teams to pull sleds, but snowmobiles are far more common today than sled dogs.

The backbone of Bush transportation is the small plane. More people own and fly their own planes in Alaska than in any other state: one in every fifty-eight Alaskans is a registered pilot. Many of their planes are floatplanes, equipped to land on lakes.

Bush pilots are the heroes of rural Alaska. They deliver supplies, mail, and passengers to remote communities and settlers. For a price, they'll carry vacationers into the roadless wilderness—and out again a day, a week, or a month later. The bush pilot Stu Ramstad is a third-generation Alaskan. "I was born into it," he said. "There were people who

Single-engine planes and snowmobiles are the transportation of choice in Alaska's interior regions.

created something where nothing existed before. That's the pioneering spirit, and that's the feeling I have."

Many Alaskans and visitors travel on the Alaska Marine Highway, a system of ferries that carry passengers and cars from port to port in southeastern, south central, and southwestern Alaska. The Alaska Railroad carries passengers and freight between Seward and Anchorage in the south and Fairbanks in the interior.

GIFTS FROM THE NATIVES

Do you have a parka? (Alaskans call it a PAR-kee.) A parka (below) is a long, warm jacket that you pull on over your head. When white explorers came to Alaska, they saw the northern Natives wearing sturdy parkas made of caribou skin. The Aleut also made such coats—out of rainproof seal intestine, perfect for their wet climate. People around the world have adopted this useful design and wear parkas made of all kinds of materials, from wool to high-tech polyester fleece and breathable nylon.

The Inupiaq, Yupik, and Aleut also gave the world the kayak (above). This is a small, flat boat with a skin cover that seals the top of the boat around the kayaker's waist to keep water out. The passenger sits on the floor and propels the sleek craft with a double-bladed paddle. Boatbuilders have copied the Native design in wood and fiberglass. Now kayakers in many countries enjoy paddling these fast-

POPULATION DENSITY

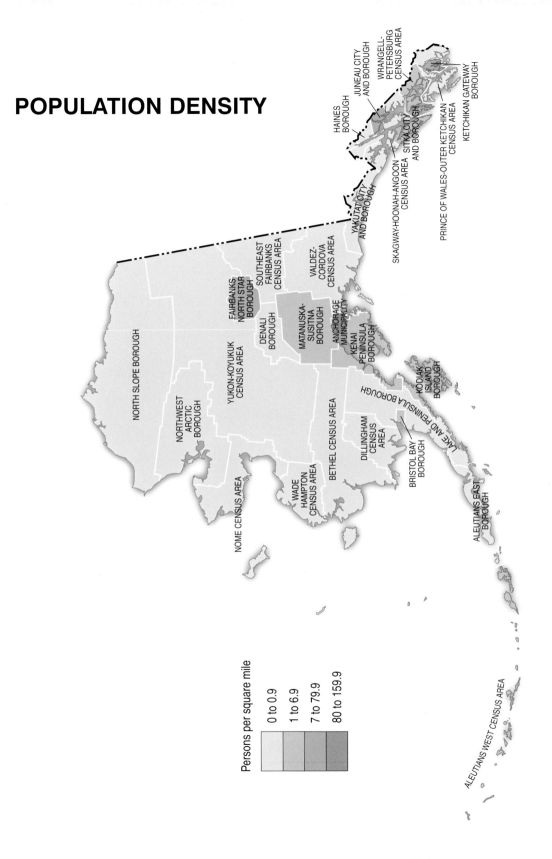

JUNEAU CITY AND BOROUGH

WRANGELL-PETERSBURG CENSUS AREA

KETCHIKAN GATEWAY BOROUGH

HAINES BOROUGH

SKAGWAY-HOONAH-ANGOON CENSUS AREA

SITKA CITY AND BOROUGH

PRINCE OF WALES-OUTER KETCHIKAN CENSUS AREA

YAKUTAT CITY AND BOROUGH

SOUTHEAST FAIRBANKS CENSUS AREA

VALDEZ-CORDOVA CENSUS AREA

FAIRBANKS NORTH STAR BOROUGH

MATANUSKA-SUSITNA BOROUGH

ANCHORAGE MUNICIPALITY

DENALI BOROUGH

KENAI PENINSULA BOROUGH

NORTH SLOPE BOROUGH

NORTHWEST ARCTIC BOROUGH

YUKON-KOYUKUK CENSUS AREA

KODIAK ISLAND BOROUGH

LAKE AND PENINSULA BOROUGH

BETHEL CENSUS AREA

DILLINGHAM CENSUS AREA

BRISTOL BAY BOROUGH

NOME CENSUS AREA

WADE HAMPTON CENSUS AREA

ALEUTIANS EAST BOROUGH

ALEUTIANS WEST CENSUS AREA

Persons per square mile

0 to 0.9
1 to 6.9
7 to 79.9
80 to 159.9

EDUCATION, ARTS, AND RECREATION

Some families live so far from the nearest settlement that children cannot go to school. To make it possible for these youngsters to get an education, in 1939 the territory began a program unlike any other in the country. It provided for children who had to study at home to receive their lessons and turn in their homework by mail. The model program continues today, using satellite television and the Internet in addition to the mail.

Most kids in Alaska, nevertheless, do attend school. For the 2004–2005 school year, 132,970 children were enrolled in public schools ranging from large high schools in Anchorage to one-room schoolhouses in small villages. Each year, more than 30,000 students are enrolled in the University of Alaska, which has campuses in Anchorage, Fairbanks, Juneau, Sitka, and Ketchikan. The university system also includes more than a dozen smaller colleges across the state, from Nome to Unalaska.

In November 2005 Governor Frank H. Murkowski asked the Alaska Legislature for an increase of $90 million for school funding, the largest funding increase in the state's history.

Education is proving to be the answer to one of Alaska's biggest social problems: brain drain. Social scientists use the term to describe what happens when large numbers of talented, educated, productive people out-migrate, or leave a place to seek opportunities elsewhere. Brain drain has been a reality for Alaska for many years. Many young people leave the state in search of jobs or education in other parts of the country. For example, a 2004 study disclosed that of all the young adults in Alaska in 1994, only 62 percent were still living in the state in 2002, compared with more than 71 percent of Alaskans as a whole.

In recent years the state government has tried to slow the flood of out-migration—and encourage excellence in high school achievement—by offering free four-year college educations in Alaska to the top 10 percent of the state's high school graduates. The program seems to be working. The same 2004 study showed that when young Alaskans went out of state to attend college, only 51 percent of them returned to live. Of those who went to college in Alaska, however, 84 percent remained in the state, contributing to an educated workforce needed for future economic developments and stability.

The arts in Alaska include everything from opera in Anchorage to traditional Eskimo dancing in Kotzebue. The larger cities have many orchestras and theaters for Western-style performing arts. Native arts, too, are a lively part of Alaska's cultural life: singers and dancers perform in the cities and at village gatherings, and artists produce fine arts and crafts, especially carvings and sculptures in wood, stone, bone, and jade, the state gem.

Alaska has no big-league sports teams, but it does have its own league of amateur baseball players, the Alaska Baseball League. Ice hockey is also popular—after all, there's plenty of ice. The Alaska Aces are a professional minor-league team. Local teams play in leagues, and major-league teams sometimes visit for games.

In general, Alaskans are athletic, outdoorsy people. Many of them fish, ski, hike, canoe, snowshoe, or ice skate. Nordic cross-country skiing is especially popular because it does not require ski lifts or resorts. Cross-country skiers can practice their sport just about anywhere there's snow on the ground. World-class cross-country trails in Anchorage and Fairbanks attract national and international races, while Mount Alyeska, near Anchorage, has hosted World Cup alpine ski races. The most "Alaskan" winter sport, however, is sled dog racing, also called mushing.

The Eskimos developed mushing as a way of traveling across snow, and early settlers learned it from them. Most people now rely on snowmobiles for serious winter transportation, but some Alaskans still run teams of husky or malamute sled dogs for work or pleasure. Each year dozens of mushing races are held all over Alaska. The most famous of these events is the Iditarod Trail Sled Dog Race, which is held every March.

Seventeen-year-old Alana Schlang trains near Mount Hood for the 150-mile Junior Iditarod Trail Sled Dog Race.

The Iitarod commemorates a historic sled dog run of 1925, when mushers raced north from Nenana to Nome with medicine to save the town from an epidemic of diphtheria. Balto, the lead dog on the team that carried the first load of medicine into Nome, became a hero.

Dogs and their mushers have to be heroic just to enter the Iditarod. They travel a 1,049-mile route from Anchorage to Nome, over mountains, burned-out stump forests, and Bering Sea ice, often during winter storms. The current record is Martin Buser's 2002 winning time of 8 days, 22 hours, 46 minutes, and 2 seconds.

The Iditarod is famous, but it has stirred up controversy in recent years. The United States Humane Society and other animal-rights groups argue that the event is too hard on the dogs. Because of their complaints, some big corporations stopped funding the race. The organizers, nevertheless, have found new sponsors in Alaska and promise to keep the Iditarod going.

Yet even some Alaskans feel that the Iditarod is just a big tourist attraction, no longer genuinely Alaskan. Mike Doogan, a lifelong Alaskan, said in the *Anchorage Daily News*, "To me the Iditarod is another piece of faux [phony] Alaskana, a sort of gigantic painted gold pan with paws." In the race's early years, a third of the participants were Natives. Now the race is more professional, with many outsiders competing. In 1995 only one Iditarod musher was a Native, although mushing was originally a Native skill. Beverly Masek, an Athabascan Indian and a former Iditarod competitor who used to be a representative in the state legislature, claims that "race organizers haven't made much effort to involve Native communities," although more Natives have participated in recent years.

The Iditarod has become a symbol for the question that some Alaskans are asking about their state: how popular can Alaska become, how much can we develop it, without losing the things that make it special?

Chapter Four

Law of the Land

Many Alaskans are passionate about politics. Political events touch their lives daily, especially because the state and federal governments control most of the land and many of the jobs in Alaska.

INSIDE GOVERNMENT

Alaska's state government is modeled on the federal government. It has three branches: the executive, the legislative, and the judicial.

Executive

The executive branch carries out the state's laws. The head of the executive branch is the governor, who is assisted by the lieutenant governor. Alaskans elect their governor and lieutenant governor every four years. No governor can serve more than two four-year terms in a row.

The governor of Alaska is one of the most powerful in the United States. He appoints all of the state's top officials, including the attorney general, all district attorneys, and the judges, and runs the fourteen major departments of the state government, including Community and Economic Development, Education and Early Development, Health and

Alaska artist R.T. Wallen created the life-size brown bear statue that sits before the State Capitol and the courts building in Juneau.

Social Services, Labor and Workforce Development, Natural Resources, and Transportation and Public Facilities.

Legislative

The legislative branch of government, called the state legislature, makes the state's laws and approves the budget, which says how the state's money will be spent (although the governor can change items in the budget). The state legislature has two houses—a senate and a house of representatives. Voters elect twenty senators for four-year terms and forty representatives for two-year terms. To vote, resident U.S. citizens must be at least eighteen years old and must have lived in

Frank H. Murkowski became Alaska's tenth governor on December 2, 2002.

Alaska for at least a year. Alaska also sends two senators and one representative to the U.S. Congress.

Unlike the rest of the states, Alaska has not been divided into counties and townships. One-third of the state is organized into fifteen boroughs. About two-thirds of the state has no organized local government at all because the population is so small and spread out. The state legislature governs this unorganized territory.

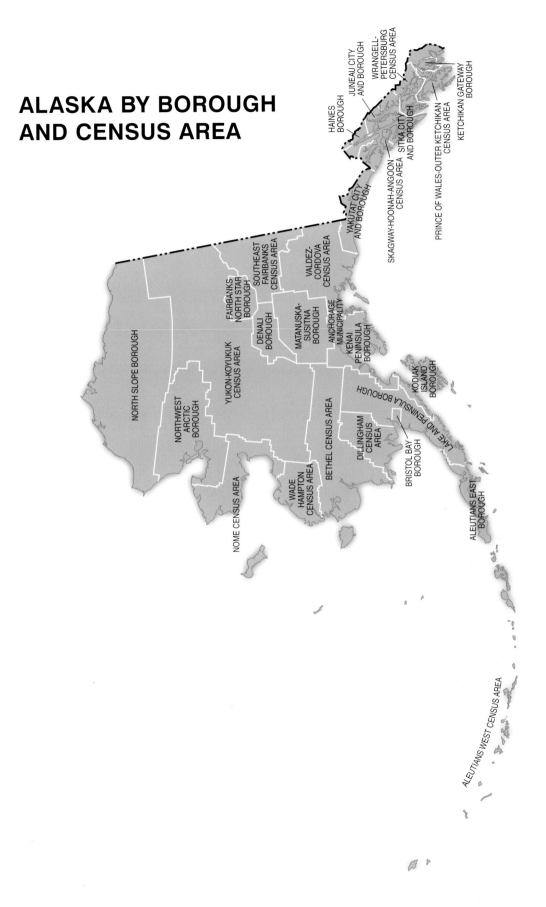

ALASKA BY BOROUGH AND CENSUS AREA

HAINES BOROUGH

JUNEAU CITY AND BOROUGH

WRANGELL-PETERSBURG CENSUS AREA

KETCHIKAN GATEWAY BOROUGH

SITKA CITY AND BOROUGH

SKAGWAY-HOONAH-ANGOON CENSUS AREA

PRINCE OF WALES-OUTER KETCHIKAN CENSUS AREA

YAKUTAT CITY AND BOROUGH

SOUTHEAST FAIRBANKS CENSUS AREA

VALDEZ-CORDOVA CENSUS AREA

FAIRBANKS NORTH STAR BOROUGH

DENALI BOROUGH

MATANUSKA-SUSITNA BOROUGH

ANCHORAGE MUNICIPALITY

NORTH SLOPE BOROUGH

NORTHWEST ARCTIC BOROUGH

YUKON-KOYUKUK CENSUS AREA

KENAI PENINSULA BOROUGH

KODIAK ISLAND BOROUGH

LAKE AND PENINSULA BOROUGH

BETHEL CENSUS AREA

DILLINGHAM CENSUS AREA

BRISTOL BAY BOROUGH

WADE HAMPTON CENSUS AREA

NOME CENSUS AREA

ALEUTIANS EAST BOROUGH

ALEUTIANS WEST CENSUS AREA

Judicial

The judicial branch upholds the law through the court system. Alaska has four levels of courts. District courts handle minor civil and criminal cases. They also issue marriage licenses. Anyone who disagrees with the verdict of a district court can appeal it, or ask for the case to be retried in a higher court.

The next level is superior court, where more serious civil and criminal cases are tried. All cases that involve children and minors are heard in a superior court. The appeals court, consisting of three judges, hears appeals from the district and superior courts. The state's highest court is the five-member supreme court. It has the final word on all appeals from the lower courts.

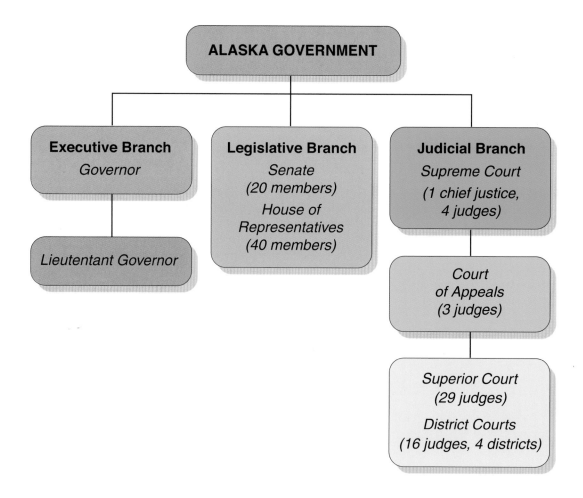

VOTERS, THE LAW, AND THE COURTS

Alaska is one of many states where voters can participate in the lawmaking process on two levels. On one level they can vote for the state legislators, who enact the state's laws. They can also take a more direct role by proposing specific laws through a process called a ballot initiative. If enough registered voters petition to have a proposed new law placed on an election ballot, that law will be put before the people of the state. If the vote goes in favor of the proposal, it becomes law. Not every proposal that gets a "yes" from the voters, however, ends up on the law books. Sometimes a newly passed law is challenged in court. That's what happened to Alaska's English-only law.

In 1998 Alaskan voters faced an initiative sponsored by organizations that wanted to make English the only language that could be used by public agencies in official government business, including education.

A voter arrives at the Ester, Alaska, polling place to cast a vote.

The initiative was aimed at immigrants, according to Tim Schultz, a spokesperson for U.S. English, one of the sponsoring groups. "When [our supporters] see people who've been in this country for fifteen or twenty years and don't know English, that bothers them," said Schultz. But Native Alaskans argued that an English-only law would discriminate against them. They pointed out that in many rural Native communities, English is a minority language, and official public business is routinely carried out in Native tongues.

The initiative passed with the support of almost 70 percent of voters. Before it could become law, however, Alaska Natives filed a lawsuit to block it. In superior court they argued that the English-only law violated their right of free speech as guaranteed in the Alaska constitution. The judge agreed, overturning the controversial law in a 2002 decision.

WHOSE STATE IS THIS?

Modern Alaska has been shaped by two important acts of the U.S. Congress. In 1971, responding to claims by Native Alaskans that they had been unfairly stripped of rights to their traditional lands, Congress passed the Alaska Native Claims Settlement Act. The act gave Eskimos, Aleuts, and Indians $925 million and title to 40 million acres of land. The federal government also created thirteen regional Native corporations and several hundred village corporations to manage the money and land that the Natives received under the settlement.

In 1980 Congress passed a bill that more than doubled the amount of federal land in Alaska. The Alaska National Interest Lands Conservation Act (ANILCA) added 56 million acres to the national wildlife refuge system, 44 million acres to the national park system, and 8 million acres to the national forest system, as well as adding parts of twenty-five rivers to the national

Conservation laws such as ANILCA have pleased nature lovers but angered some Alaskans.

wild and scenic river system. Lovers of wilderness everywhere rejoiced. Many Alaskans, though, complained that too much of their state had been removed from local control. In both Alaska and Washington, D.C., interested people continue to debate the future of these lands.

Alaskan politics can be very complicated. Many federal, state, and local agencies, boards, and officials may be involved in making a single decision. Buying land is a good example of how Alaska is different from other states. The easiest way to get land is to buy it from someone who already owns it. Less than 1 percent of the land in Alaska, however, belongs to private owners.

Most of this land is located in towns or along roads. Because these sites are easy to reach, they are considered the most desirable land in the state—and the prices go steadily up.

Federal homesteading programs, which gave free land to anyone willing to settle and work on it, ended in Alaska in 1986. The state does allow people to buy some state-owned land through a lottery system. "It isn't easy to get land here," said a woman who moved to Alaska with her husband, seven children, and twenty goats in 1974, "but it's possible."

Two-thirds of Alaska, about 387,000 square miles, is federal land. Some of this land is set aside for military bases. Enormous tracts of it, especially in the southwest, west, and northeast, are national wildlife refuges. The rest of the public land is controlled by the Bureau of Land Management, the National Forest Service, or the National Park Service.

Some people already lived on lands that ANILCA brought under federal control as public lands. They were allowed to keep their properties, so private holdings are scattered throughout public land. Still, the U.S. government is the state's biggest landowner. "Alaska is kind of weird that way," said J. Scott Feierabend, an official with the National Wildlife Federation in Anchorage. "Since most of it is federal land, the state's major policy issues are going to be decided by the Lower Forty-eight." This makes some Alaskans bitter. One told a reporter, "What bugs me is that when decisions are made about Alaska, people from Texas and Ohio, California and New York carry more weight than people from Alaska."

People who live and work on Alaska's government-owned lands often resent the rules they must follow. Residents of the small settlement of Chisana, in the Wrangell–Saint Elias National Preserve, met with Park Service workers to air their complaints. They grumbled about limits on hunting and about the permits they had to get before they could put up new buildings.

One resident told a park worker, "Because of all the demands you people make, soon there will be nobody here, just the way you want it." Another man, who arranges trips for hunters and other visitors, said, "You call this public land, but pretty soon nobody will be able to use it but the Park Service."

A Park Service official had a different view: "Wilderness is disappearing faster than people think," he said. "Wrangell–Saint Elias is a treasure worth preserving, a large intact ecosystem rarely found anymore. We see ourselves as bankers, saving it for the future." Fred Ewan, an elderly Native whose people have lived in the region for thousands of years, agreed: "It's good they made the park," he told a reporter. "Good for the animals. There were too many people shooting them."

Wrangell–Saint Elias is a designated World Heritage site. To preserve its natural beauty and flora and fauna, limits have been placed on hunting and building.

LAND-USE ISSUES

Many of the most hotly debated political issues in Alaska concern the land and its resources. On one side are those who want to protect the land and its creatures so that the wilderness will be there for future generations. On the other side are those who believe that it is better to use such resources as timber, oil, and minerals to create jobs and profits now. Some of these issues are decided at the state level, but because so much of Alaska is federal land, the U.S. government and the courts must often try to balance the views of environmentalists with those of business interests.

Two of the hardest-fought battles concern the Tongass National Forest in southeastern Alaska and the Arctic National Wildlife Refuge in the far north. The Tongass is the largest national forest in the United States. It covers 17 million acres, making it about the size of the state of West Virginia. A rain forest, the Tongass sometimes gets as much as two hundred inches of precipitation in a year. It is the last big, unbroken stretch of rain forest in the temperate zone, the part of the earth that lies between the tropics and the polar regions.

Although parts of the Tongass National Forest have been logged, much of it remains untouched—but perhaps not for long. During the 1990s most of the Tongass was protected by the so-called roadless rule, a federal decision that banned the creation of new roads in 60 million acres of national forests. Timber industries protested the rule, and in 2003 President George W. Bush lifted it, opening the way for the construction of up to one thousand miles of new logging roads in the forest. Timber industry advisers point to the need for jobs in Alaska and to the worldwide demand for wood and paper products. They claim that their plan for logging the Tongass will leave large stretches of the forest untouched. Biologists, however, fear that the combination of road building and logging will chop the forest into small parcels and clog streams with the soil that erodes from clear-cut hillsides. They also oppose the logging of the Tongass's largest old-growth trees, some of which are six hundred years old. The battle over the Tongass will no doubt continue as both sides make their arguments to Congress and the courts.

Another conflict rages over the Arctic National Wildlife Refuge (ANWR), a 19.6-million-acre area of northeastern Alaska that is also managed by the federal government. Parts of the refuge are protected as wilderness. However, under the 1980 Alaska National Interest Lands Conservation Act, the northern part of the refuge was given a lesser level of protection. Under

Greenpeace activists protest the cutting of trees in Tongass National Forest.

ANILCA, the U.S. Congress could allow oil and gas exploration and drilling in this part of the refuge. The majority of Alaskans favor opening ANWR, believing that drilling there will help their state's economy and ease the nation's dependence on foreign oil.

A district of the refuge called Area 1002 is at the heart of the debate. This 1.5-million-acre zone is a vital part of the habitat of two huge populations of caribou, the Central Arctic and Porcupine herds.

This aerial view shows the migration of caribou in the Arctic National Wildlife Refuge. Herds in this region contain thousands of animals.

It is also, according to energy-industry scientists, the part of the refuge most likely to contain oil and natural gas. Although environmentalists and others who oppose drilling in the ANWR plan to continue their fight in the courts, it is most likely that drilling will eventually take place. It remains to be seen what effect such activities will have on the ANWR's wildlife.

The Arctic National Wildlife Refuge is not one of Alaska's leading tourist attractions—according to the refuge's management, fewer than

BENNY BENSON'S FLAG

Alaska's state flag was created decades before Alaska became a state. In 1927 the Territory of Alaska held a contest for schoolchildren to design a territorial flag. Benny Benson, a thirteen-year-old Aleut seventh grader, turned in the winning entry.

Benny Benson's design was a blue background with eight gold stars: the North Star and the constellation that many call the Big Dipper but others call the Great Bear. Said Benny, "The blue field is for the Alaska sky and the forget-me-not, an Alaska flower. The North Star is for the future state of Alaska, the most northerly of the Union. The Great Bear—symbolizing strength." His flag flew over the Territory of Alaska until 1959, when Alaska became a state. On July 4, 1959, when the flag was raised in the new state capital for the first time, Benny Benson led a parade carrying his flag.

1,500 people visit it in a typical year. But is a unique ecosystem, and it is also the home of Native peoples who have lived off that land for generations. In the 2001 book *Arctic Refuge: A Circle of Testimony*, a member of the Gwich'in community described the importance of the caribou that live in the ANWR: "As I was growing up . . . I never thought that our way of life would be threatened or could be lost. . . . I hope with all my heart that my children will have the caribou there for them too. . . . I cannot bear to think that we can lose all this in one sweep of a vote miles away from our homelands." This Native spokesperson, like other Alaskans, must face the fact that many decisions about Alaska's fate lie in federal hands.

Chapter Five

Making a Living

At the end of the nineteenth century, people flocked to Alaska seeking fortunes in gold. Today very few Alaskans expect to strike it rich by prospecting. Most are simply looking for a reliable way to earn a living in a state that has weathered its share of economic troubles.

CHANGING WITH THE TIMES

Throughout the nineteenth and twentieth centuries Alaska's economy depended largely on natural resources, which meant that it had a "boom and bust" economy. When world prices for Alaska's resources were high, the state prospered. When prices dropped, the state suffered. The economic rollercoaster of the 1980s—a burst of prosperity followed by a sharp slump because of rapid changes in oil prices—showed Alaskans the drawbacks of relying so heavily on mineral resources to drive their economy.

Like many other places, Alaska is now trying to create a more balanced economy by developing such other industries as manufacturing, services, and retail sales. At present, though, Alaska's economy rests on three legs: oil, tourism, and fish. Unemployment remains a nagging problem.

With ocean surrounding Alaska on three sides, commercial fishing contributes 5 percent to the gross state product of Alaska.

Many people cannot find jobs, and some jobs last for just one season. Industries such as fishing and tourism, for example, hire workers in summer and lay them off in winter.

To sustain its economy, Alaska looks to expand other sectors, such as retail and services.

ALASKA WORKFORCE

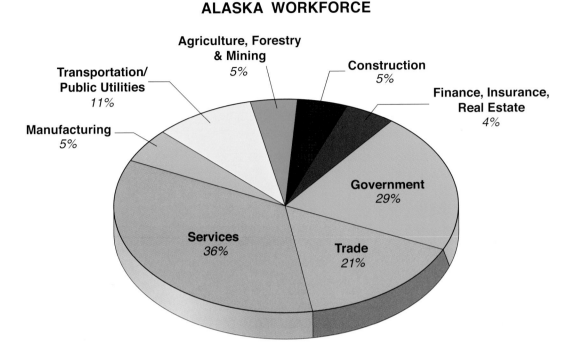

WORKING ON LAND AND SEA

Government is one of the single largest employers in Alaska. About 29 percent of the workforce is employed directly by the federal, state, or local government. In addition, many jobs in the construction industry come from government projects.

Although only about eight thousand Alaskans actually work in the petroleum industry, oil is vital to the state's economy. Oil companies pay state taxes on the oil and gas they drill on the Kenai Peninsula and the North Slope, and Alaska also receives a share of the money the companies make when they sell the oil. About eighty-five cents of every dollar of state money derives from oil. Alaska also has lead, coal, zinc, gold, silver, platinum, and tin mines. Some scientists think that large reserves of coal and other resources remain to be discovered under the Alaskan soil.

Tourism was launched in Alaska in the 1890s, when passenger ships began cruising the Inside Passage. In 2003, 1.4 million people visited Alaska, according to the Alaska Humanities Forum. Half of those visitors were passengers on cruise ships that docked at the towns of the southeastern coast. In all, tourists spent $1.5 billion in Alaska that year, accounting for 5 percent of the gross state product (the value of all goods and services sold in the state). Tourism creates about 25,000 jobs in Alaska. Most of them, though, are low paying.

Alaska's commercial fisheries produce more seafood than those of any other state, and they contribute about 5 percent of the state's gross product. But fishing, like the oil industry, has busts as well as booms.

The cruise tour industry contributes to Alaska's economy.

A fishing boat near Ketchikan hauls a large catch of salmon.

"I'm on the verge of collapse," said salmon fisherman Ross Mullins of Cordova in 1994. "And in my mind, and the minds of most fishermen down here, there's no question what the causal fact is." Mullins and many other fishermen in Prince William Sound blamed the 1989 Exxon oil spill for a disastrous slump in salmon prices, saying that the spill made people afraid to eat Alaskan salmon. Others, however, have pointed out that the price of salmon on the world market has gone up and down many times. In recent years salmon raised on fish farms in Canada, Chile, Norway, and the Lower 48 states has competed well in the marketplace with wild-caught Alaskan salmon. In addition, federal limits on salmon fishing, designed to prevent overharvesting of the wild fish populations, have sharply cut into the profits of many commercial fishers. In order to protect its wild fish, Alaska has outlawed fish farming in its waters.

In the 1980s Alaska's commercial fishing boats began harvesting a new marine product: pollack and other fish scooped from the depths of the Bering Sea. Most of these fish are processed into a product called surimi, which is marketed as imitation crabmeat. Alaskans also fish the Bering Sea for real crabs, including the huge, long-legged king crabs.

Commercial farming is centered in the valleys of the Tanana and Matanuska rivers. The major crops are hay (for feeding livestock), potatoes, barley, oats, and vegetables. Long summer days and mild temperatures produce Alaska's famous giant vegetables, such as 90-pound cabbages.

Some 70,000 Alaskans, mostly Natives, follow a way of life called subsistence. They live off the land—hunting, fishing, and farming—and they produce as much of their own food, clothing, and other goods as possible. When they need money to buy something they can't make themselves, they earn a few dollars by panning for gold or trapping for furs to sell.

A farmer poses with her giant cabbage at the Alaska State Fair.

Many Alaskans, such as this woman picking berries, live off the land, at least in part.

A number of Alaskans still practice small-time mining. One man spends his summers with his wife and daughter in a small wooden cabin north of the Wrangell Mountains. He works a gold claim on Bonanza Creek and splits his finds with the owner of the claim, who lives in Anchorage. "An ounce of gold is a good day for us," the miner said. "It's not much money for all the hardship, but I consider it a privilege to be out here." His fourteen-year-old daughter said, "Mom says this experience will make a better person of me."

Few people in Alaska can successfully adopt the subsistence way of life, but even those with steady jobs may boost their incomes with a little trapping or gold panning. A great many residents grow their own vegetables, and they stock their freezers with meat they've hunted, fish they've caught, and berries they've picked. Modern Alaskans still have something in common with the first Alaskans, who lived off the land.

EARNING A LIVING

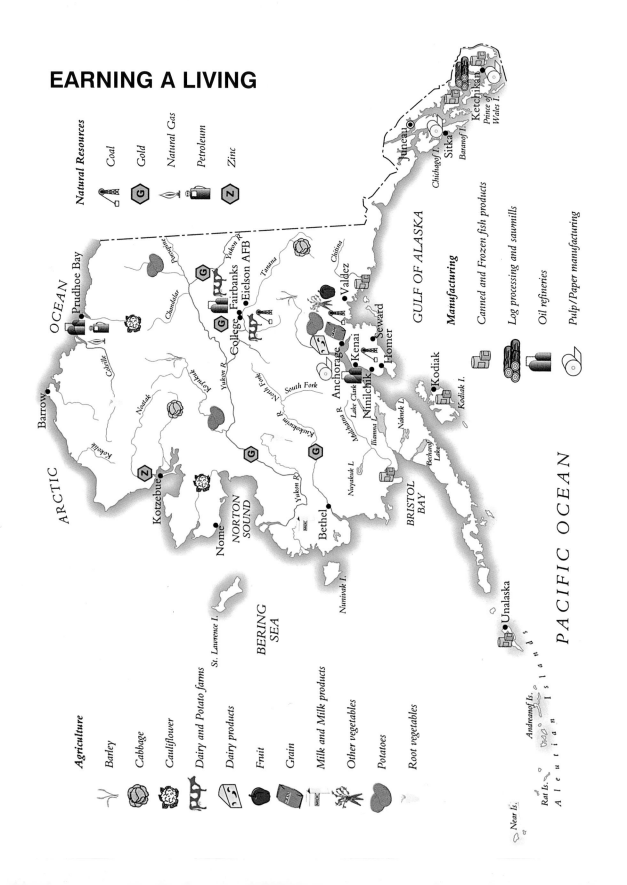

Natural Resources

- Coal
- Gold (G)
- Natural Gas
- Petroleum
- Zinc (Z)

Manufacturing

- Canned and Frozen fish products
- Log processing and sawmills
- Oil refineries
- Pulp/Paper manufacturing

Agriculture

- Barley
- Cabbage
- Cauliflower
- Dairy and Potato farms
- Dairy products
- Fruit
- Grain
- Milk and Milk products
- Other vegetables
- Potatoes
- Root vegetables

ARCTIC OCEAN

GULF OF ALASKA

PACIFIC OCEAN

BERING SEA

NORTON SOUND

BRISTOL BAY

Prudhoe Bay
Barrow
Kotzebue
Nome
Bethel
Unalaska
Fairbanks
College
Eielson AFB
Valdez
Kenai
Anchorage
Ninilchik
Homer
Seward
Kodiak
Juneau
Sitka
Ketchikan

Prince of Wales I.
Baranof I.
Chichagof I.
Kodiak I.
Nunivak I.
St. Lawrence I.

Colville
Chandalar
Noatak
Kobuk
Yukon R.
Porcupine
Tanana
Chitina
Kuskokwim R.
North Fork
South Fork
Mulchatna R.
Lake Clark
Iliamna L.
Naknek L.
Becharof Lake
Nuyakuk L.

Aleutian Islands
Near Is.
Rat Is.
Andreanof Is.

SIX STATE FAIRS

Alaska is so big that it needs more than one state fair. It has six. Every year state fairs are held in Palmer, in the Matanuska River valley; in Fairbanks; in Ninilchik, on the Kenai Peninsula; in Haines, in the southeast; in Kodiak; and in Delta Junction. Only the Palmer and Fairbanks fairs are recognized by the state as "official" state fairs, but all of them offer a good time to residents and visitors.

"The best part of a fair is that it's fun," said Deidra Berberich, one of the managers of the Palmer fair. "It's a great atmosphere. The kids are jumping with excitement. Everyone shows up in a good mood. And when they leave, they're tired, but you can tell they had a good time." Palmer's festival honors the Matanuska valley's history as Alaska's prime farmland with livestock and vegetable shows. It also features Native events, including Alutiiq dancers from Kodiak and such contests as

2003 GROSS STATE PRODUCT: $32 Million

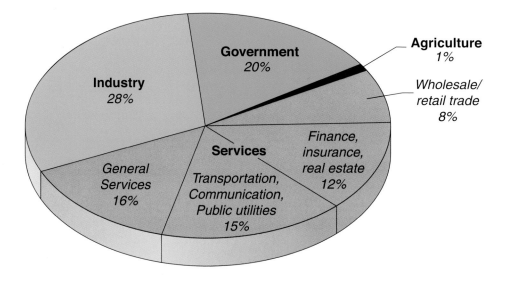

THE COST OF LIVING

In some ways Alaskans pride themselves on being set apart from the rest of the country. Many of them moved to this northern state in search of independence, even isolation. At the same time they pay a price for the remoteness of their home.

Things made in the Lower 48—everything from cars to comic books—cost more in Alaska because they have to be shipped so far. Travel is expensive, too. "It takes a major investment to visit the lower states, or anywhere else, for that matter," said Nancy Carlson, who lives with her large family in the interior. A growing number of Alaskans, however, are able to save money by shopping online or at large warehouse-type stores, such as Costco.

The cost of living is high, but so is the average Alaskan's income. In 2004 the state was ranked fourteenth in the nation in average income per person. One source of money that everyone counts on is the Permanent Fund dividend. The state set up the fund to invest money so that when the North Slope oil fields run dry, there will be a source of income to replace them. Every year, Alaska gives part of the interest on that investment fund to people who have lived in the state for at least one full year. In 2005 each qualified resident received a check for $845.76.

In the early 2000s about 9 percent of Alaska's population lived below the poverty line, compared with 12 percent in the country as a whole. More of Alaska's poor dwell in rural areas than in the cities, but poverty and homelessness are growing problems for Anchorage and other population centers.

Twenty-five-year-old Dan Goodell was born in Alaska and lives in Anchorage. He works in a restaurant during the winter and a fish cannery during the summer. Goodell summed up the feelings of many Alaskans when he said, "A lot of people in the Lower Forty-Eight dream of coming up here to live. They have this fantasy that Alaska is some kind of frontier wonderland. It *is* a wonderful place—if you've got some money. But there are a lot of people here looking for work. If you're not making it down south, Alaska isn't the answer to your problems."

Sale items entice shoppers into an otherwise expensive market.

Chapter Six

By Land, Sea, and Air

There's much to see in Alaska—but to see it all, visitors have to travel by land, sea, and air, and they have to cover a whole *lot* of territory. "I was born in Alaska and I've been back eight times with my family," said seventeen-year-old Jason Valentine. "But still we've only seen a tiny part of what's up there."

Many visitors start a tour of Alaska with a trip north along the Inside Passage aboard a ferry or cruise ship.

UP THE INSIDE PASSAGE

Traveling the Inside Passage is taking a trip through Alaska's history. As you travel the Passage, you'll see Native arts, Russian buildings, gold rush relics, and a modern state capital, Juneau. Ketchikan, at the south end of the Passage, has the world's largest collection of totem poles, the work of Tlingit and Haida artisans. Petersburg, a fishing town settled by people from Norway, still has many buildings decorated with traditional Norwegian carved and painted designs called rosemaling. Each May residents of Petersburg hold a Little Norway Festival.

Hikers experience Alaska up close.

At the Totem Heritage Center and Nature Park in Ketchikan, there are totem poles as much as 185 years old.

Sitka was the center of Aleksandr Baranov's Russian-American empire. Today it is one of many places in southern Alaska where visitors can see Russian churches with their onion-shaped domes. The largest of these churches, Saint Michael's Cathedral, has a famous collection of Russian religious paintings known as icons. In Sitka travelers can see the New Archangel Dancers perform traditional Russian dances and afterward can wander through the old Russian cemetery.

Although Alaskans have often considered moving their capital to an easier-to-reach location near Anchorage, the southeastern coastal city of Juneau remains the center of state government. It is also the site of the Alaska State Museum, which has a large collection of Native items, and the Juneau-Douglas City Museum, which explains the history of gold mining in the region. "It helps to be a mountain goat in Juneau," said the travel writer Suzanne Hopkins. The city's streets aren't quite as hard to climb as the slopes where mountain goats roam, but Alaska's capital is built on the slopes of several steep hills.

Juneau, which started as a gold camp, is close to some of the most magnificent natural wonders of the Inside Passage. Helicopters carry tourists to the nearby Mendenhall Glacier, where visitors can walk on the ice sheet. In Glacier Bay National Park people watch from cruise ships—or from kayaks, if they're feeling adventurous—as huge chunks of ice break free from tidewater glaciers. Whales often surface near the boats.

Several trails at Mendenhall Glacier allow for breathtaking photographs. One trail is even named Photo Point Trail.

Exploring the ice-packed waterway of Glacier Bay by kayak is one way to explore.

Haines and Skagway, at the north end of the Passage, have road connections to the Alaska Highway. Haines is famous for the 3,500 or so bald eagles that gather there every winter to feed on salmon in the Chilkat River. It is the largest gathering of eagles in the world. Skagway was the gateway to the Yukon during the gold rush at the close of the nineteenth century. The Klondike Gold Rush National Historical Park preserves the history of those wild and woolly days. Following the route taken by many prospectors on their way to the Yukon, visitors ride an old-fashioned train on an exciting and scenic trip over the White Pass.

SOUTH CENTRAL AND ANCHORAGE

Northwest of the Inside Passage is Wrangell–Saint Elias National Park. Six times bigger than Yellowstone, this park contains the largest wilderness area in the United States: 13.2 million acres, nearly twice the size of New Jersey. The park also has nine of the highest peaks in the country and dozens of glaciers. Within the park is the old Kennecott Copper Mine, once one of Alaska's major mines. The Park Service now owns the major structure of the mine and is developing the site as a tourist attraction.

"Many of these valleys were filled with ice, and not very long ago," explained the glacier expert Ed LaChappelle. "The cool northern climate here delayed its disappearance, and glaciers are receding as the great ice sheets did

Across Disenchantment Bay in Wrangell–Saint Elias National Park is Hubbard Glacier.

before them. So if you want a glimpse of what New York and Wisconsin were like 12,000 years ago, you can see it here." On his first visit to the park, the travel writer Noel Grove said, "I can't get over the feeling that I'm the last person on earth. Or maybe the first."

Farther west is Anchorage, the modern city that boasts that it is "only half an hour from Alaska." Icebergs, glaciers, Native villages, gold mines, and wildlife refuges are all close at hand. From downtown you can see Denali on the horizon. The mountain is so big that it looks close, but it is actually 150 miles away.

Anchorage has changed much since it began in 1914 as a cluster of tents for workers on the Alaska Railroad. Bob Atwood, who used to publish the *Anchorage Times*, recalled early days in the city: "A dirt road

Though a modern city, Anchorage is surrounded by stunning wilderness.

ran around Anchorage. If you wanted to take a Sunday drive, you literally had to go around in circles." Now Anchorage, like other large cities, has problems with suburban sprawl and smog. But it also has many of Alaska's cultural attractions, such as the Alaska Museum of Natural History, the Alaska Zoo, the Alaska Public Lands Information Center, the Alaska Native Heritage Center, and the Anchorage Museum of History and Art. Earthquake Park commemorates the fearsome quake of March 27, 1964, when parts of downtown sank thirty feet. The Oomingmak Musk Ox Producers' Co-op sells garments knitted by western Alaska Natives from qiviut, the soft underwool of musk oxen.

Visitors in Anchorage in February get a chance to take part in one of Alaska's biggest festivals, the Anchorage Fur Rendezvous. The rendezvous began in 1936 to give fur trappers a place to sell their furs. Now it's a ten-day, citywide party that includes sled dog races on downtown streets and snowshoe baseball games.

South of Anchorage, on Kachemak Bay near the tip of the Kenai Peninsula, is the little town of Homer. Many artists have settled in cabins or houseboats in this picturesque community, with views of the ocean and the mountains. Homer has a number of art galleries and jewelry and craft shops, as well as the Pratt Museum, which contains exhibits about the area's history and wildlife. The bay is famed as a fishing spot. Sport fishers come from around the world to catch its giant halibut.

Also located on the Kenai Peninsula is the city of Seward, 126 miles south of Anchorage. With 3,022-foot Mount Marathon at its back and the sea at its doorstep, Seward is a popular spot for recreation and fishing. It contains the terminal for the Alaska Railroad, the gateway to Kenai Fjords National Park, and the site of a challenging footrace up Mount Marathon every Fourth of July.

THE SOUTHWEST

To many visitors, southwest Alaska means Kodiak Island. People visit Kodiak to see the famous Kodiak brown bears—most often viewed from the air during "flightseeing" trips. The town of Old Harbor, the site of the first Russian settlement in America, has an Eastern Orthodox Church more than two hundred years old. The Alutiiq Museum and Archaeological Repository in Kodiak, which opened in 1995, is dedicated to preserving the heritage of the Alutiiq people, who have lived on the island for 7,500 years.

In Katmai National Park on the Alaska Peninsula, you'll find the Valley of Ten Thousand Smokes. After a volcano erupted there in 1912, vents in the valley floor spewed out steam hot enough to melt metal. Today only a

Russian influences can still be seen on Kodiak Island.

few vents remain active. Katmai also has forests, rivers, lakes, glaciers, and plenty of brown bears. The park can be reached only by air. There are almost no roads in southwestern Alaska. Ferries carry passengers to Kodiak Island and to several ports on the Alaska Peninsula and the Aleutian Islands. But ferry service ends at Unalaska and Akutan, at the beginning of the Aleutian chain. People who want to go to the thinly populated islands must travel by private boat or plane.

The Bristol Bay area and the Yukon-Kuskokwim Delta villages are the most populous and economically important parts of southwestern Alaska. Dillingham and Bethel, the largest cities, are surrounded by Native Yupik villages.

TEN LARGEST CITIES

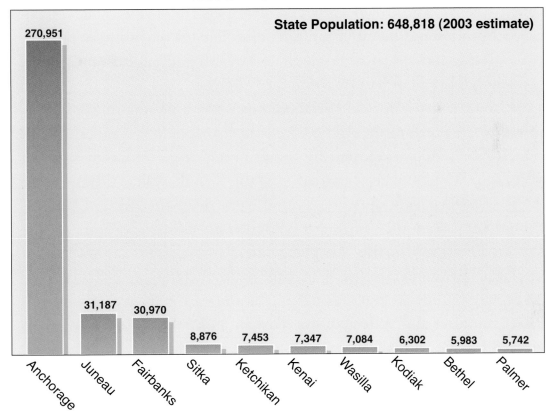

State Population: 648,818 (2003 estimate)

City	Population
Anchorage	270,951
Juneau	31,187
Fairbanks	30,970
Sitka	8,876
Ketchikan	7,453
Kenai	7,347
Wasilla	7,084
Kodiak	6,302
Bethel	5,983
Palmer	5,742

NORTH TO THE FUTURE

Nome, the biggest city in northwestern Alaska, is reachable only by air. Once there, however, visitors can drive a rental car along 250 miles of roads in the area, looking for bears, musk oxen, and other wildlife. They can also pan for gold on the very beaches where the great gold rush started or take a short flight to eastern Russia. Because more than half of Nome's population is Yupik, the city's shops are a good place to buy the clothing, jewelry, and carvings these Natives make. The Carrie M. McLain Memorial Museum houses exhibits about Yupik culture and Nome's gold rush.

The northernmost town in the United States is Barrow, located in the North Slope Borough on the coast of the Arctic Sea. With a population of just under 4,700 at the end of 2004, Barrow is a fairly small town—but it has grown considerably since the 1970s. The North Slope Borough has invested millions of dollars of oil-industry taxes in roads, water and electrical services, and health and education for local residents, more than half of whom are Natives.

Kobuk Valley National Park contains something one might be surprised to see north of the Arctic Circle: twenty-five square miles of sand dunes. The sand was created by the grinding of glaciers thousands of years ago. Wind and river carried it to the Kobuk Valley. Gates, of the Arctic National Park and Preserve, also north of the Arctic Circle, is sometimes called the "ultimate wilderness." It includes part of the Brooks Range and marks the place where forest gives way to tundra. Caribou outnumber humans in this majestic landscape. The Arctic National Wildlife Refuge, farther north and east, gets even fewer visitors. "But after all," reflected one Alaskan park ranger, "the refuge was created for the animals, not for us."

Some of the dunes at Kobuk Valley National Park stand as high as 150 feet.

PLACES TO SEE

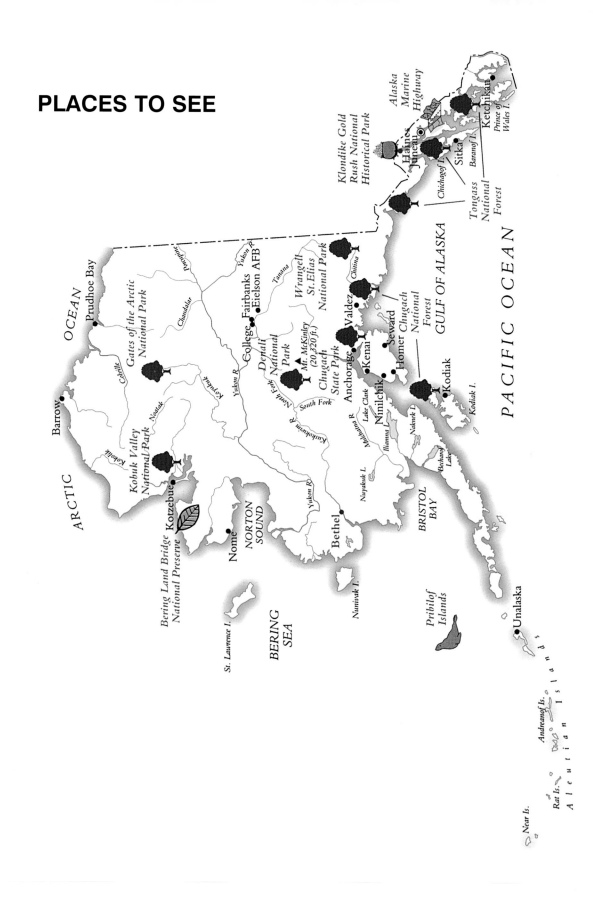

Alaska Marine Highway

Klondike Gold Rush National Historical Park

Haines
Juneau

Ketchikan
Prince of Wales I.

Chichagof I.
Baranof I.
Sitka

Tongass National Forest

PACIFIC OCEAN

GULF OF ALASKA

Chitina

Wrangell St. Elias National Park

Valdez

Chugach National Forest

Seward
Homer
Chugach State Park
Anchorage
Kenai
Ninilchik

OCEAN

Prudhoe Bay

Gates of the Arctic National Park

Colville

Putuligma

Chandalar

Yukon R.
Fairbanks
College
Eielson AFB
Tanana

Denali National Park

▲ Mt. McKinley (20,320 ft.)

North Fork

South Fork

Kuskokwim R.

Mulchatna R.
Lake Clark
Iliamna L.
Nuyakuk L.

Kodiak
Kodiak I.

Naknek L.

BRISTOL BAY

Becharof Lake

ARCTIC

Barrow

Kobuk

Kobuk Valley National Park

Noatak

Bering Land Bridge National Preserve
Kotzebue

Nome

NORTON SOUND

Bethel

Yukon R.

Nunivak I.

St. Laurence I.

BERING SEA

Pribilof Islands

Unalaska

Near Is.

Rat Is.
Andreanof Is.
Aleutian Islands

THE HEART OF ALASKA

Fairbanks, Alaska's second-largest city, is the population center of the interior. The Alaska Highway leads thousands of visitors a year to Fairbanks and the smaller communities around it. The city's attractions include a forty-four-acre theme park called Alaskaland, the University of Alaska Museum, and the Milepost, a monument in downtown Fairbanks that shows the distances to such far-off points as Paris and Mexico City.

From Fairbanks, travelers can drive to Dawson (formerly Dawson City) in Canada's Yukon Territory, to the Arctic Circle and beyond on the road to Prudhoe Bay, or to Anchorage and Valdez in the south. Most visitors head south. On the way to Anchorage, motorists stop at Alaska's number-one tourist attraction, Denali National Park, hoping for a cloud-free glimpse of the highest peak in North America. The mountain, once named for William McKinley, twenty-fifth president of the United States, is now called by its Athabascan name, Denali, which means "the high one."

The park is both tundra and taiga (TIE-guh), or evergreen forest. It is home to caribou, grizzly bears, moose, wolves, and other animals. Alaskans and the National Park Service are debating making changes in how the park is run. For now, the number of vehicles and people that can enter the park on any given day is limited. Park rangers believe that limits are needed to give visitors a chance to see wildlife up close and to feel the solitude and natural beauty of the wilderness. "I don't mind waiting to get in," said an eleven-year-old girl from California in 1994. "I don't even mind that we didn't get a look at the big mountain. I'd come back here every year if my mom and dad would bring me."

Denali National Park is home to North America's highest peak, glaciers, lakes, and an abundance of wildlife.

Many people who have visited Alaska feel the same way. And most of those who live there love their state. They want it to grow and prosper, and they worry about protecting the land and its resources. "Alaskans don't see the value of order, don't see the value of looking to the future," one Anchorage woman said in the 1970s, fearing that Anchorage's fast-growing sprawl of trailer parks and shopping malls would spread to other parts of the state.

It is hard for some Alaskans to understand that people all over the country and the world, even those who have never visited Alaska, also care very much about the big, unspoiled state and what happens there. "Maybe I'll never live in Alaska," said Zachary Harris of Portland, Oregon, "but I need to know that it's there, that it's one place we won't mess up. It belongs to all of us."

People who do see "the great land" never forget it. The geographer Henry Gannett, who surveyed Alaska in 1904 for the federal government, wrote, "Its grandeur is more valuable than the gold or the fish or the timber, for it will never be exhausted."

THE FLAG: *There are a total of eight stars on the flag's blue background. Seven gold stars, in the shape of the Big Dipper, represent Alaska's gold resources. The eighth star, alone in the upper right-hand corner, stands for Alaska's location in the far north. Alaska's flag was adopted in 1927.*

THE SEAL: *The symbols on the seal represent Alaska's agriculture, fishing, and mining. The seal also includes images of snow-covered mountains and the northern lights. Alaska's state seal was adopted in 1913, long before Alaska actually became a state.*

State Survey

Statehood: January 3, 1959

Origin of Name: *Alaska* probably comes from the Russian version of the Aleutian word *alyeska,* meaning "peninsula," "the great land," or "land that is not an island."

Nickname: Land of the Midnight Sun, The Last Frontier

Capital: Juneau

Motto: North to the Future

Bird: Willow ptarmigan

Fish: King salmon

Flower: Forget-me-not

Tree: Sitka spruce

Gem: Jade

Willow ptarmigan

Forget-me-not

ALASKA'S FLAG

The poem "Alaska's Flag," by Marie Drake, was published in the Alaska School Bulletin in 1935. Five years later her verses were set to music by Elinor Dusenberry. In 1955 "Alaska's Flag" was adopted as the official state song.

Words by Marie Drake

Music by Elinor Dusenberry

GEOGRAPHY

Highest Point: 20,320 feet above sea level, at Denali (Mount McKinley)

Lowest Point: Sea level

Area: 656,425 square miles, including 17,502 square miles of inland water, but excluding 27,355 square miles of coastal water

Greatest Distance North to South: Approximately 1,390 miles

Greatest Distance East to West: Approximately 2,210 miles

Borders: The country of Canada lies to the east, the Arctic Ocean to the north, the Bering Sea to the west, and the Pacific Ocean to the south

Hottest Recorded Temperature: 100°F at Fort Yukon on June 27, 1915

Coldest Recorded Temperature: −80°F at Prospect Creek Camp, near Stevens Village, on January 23, 1971

Average Annual Precipitation: 21.5 inches

Major Rivers: Alsek, Chitina, Colville, Copper, Kobuk, Kuskokwim, Noatak, Selawik, Yukon

Major Lakes: Becharof, Clark, Iliamna, Minchumina, Naknek, Skilak, Teshekpuk, Tustumena

Trees: Birch, black spruce, cottonwood, Sitka spruce, western hemlock, white spruce, willow

Wild Plants: Anemone, dwarf rhododendron, forget-me-not, lupine, marsh marigold, paintbrush

Animals: Arctic reindeer, beaver, black bear, caribou, coyote, Dall sheep, grizzly bear, Kodiak brown bear, marten, mink, moose, mountain goat, otter, red fox, Sitka black-tailed deer, wolf

Mountain goat

Birds: Bald eagle, duck, golden eagle, goose, grouse, hawk, loon, ptarmigan, puffin, snowy owl, surfbird, tundra swan

Fish and Oceanic Mammals: Brook trout, chinook, cod, crab, halibut, harbor seal, herring, king salmon, lake trout, northern pike, pink salmon, polar bear, porpoise, rainbow trout, sea lion, sea otter, shrimp, walrus, whale

Endangered Animals: Blue whale, Eskimo curlew, sea lion, short-tailed albatross, leatherback sea turtle

Sea lion

TIMELINE

Alaskan History

c. 12,000 BCE–7000 BCE Ancestors of Athabascan Indians cross the Bering land bridge to Alaska.

c. 7000 BCE–4000 BCE Eskimos and Aleuts migrate to Alaska from Siberia and Arctic Canada.

1728 Vitus Bering passes north through the Bering Strait, proving that Asia and North America are separate.

1741 On another expedition to explore northeastern Siberia, Bering sails into the Gulf of Alaska and lands on Kayak Island.

1778 British captain James Cook surveys the Alaskan coast.

1784 Russians make a settlement at Three Saints Bay on Kodiak Island.

1792 Captain George Vancouver, a British navigator, charts the southeast corner of Alaska.

1799 Russia grants a monopoly of the Alaska fur trade to the Russian-American Company.

1823 Father Ivan Veniaminov, a Russian missionary, begins working among the Aleuts.

1867 Secretary of state William Seward purchases Alaska from Russia for the United States for $7.2 million.

1878 First two commercial salmon canneries are built at Klawock, near Sitka.

1884 District of Alaska is created.

1896 Gold discovered in Klondike River basin of Canadian Yukon; unsuccessful prospectors in the Yukon turn toward Alaska, where some gold is found around Nome in 1898 and around Fairbanks in 1902.

1906 Alaska is allowed to send an elected delegate, without a vote, to Congress.

1912 Alaska is organized as a territory of the United States.

1917 Mount McKinley National Park, now Denali National Park, is established.

1924 Lieutenant Carl Ben Eielson flies first airmail to Alaska.

1942 During World War II the Japanese invade and occupy the two westernmost Aleutian Islands.

1943 Construction is completed on the Alaska Highway, connecting Dawson Creek in Canada's British Columbia province to the city of Fairbanks, Alaska.

1948–1984 Because of the cold war with the Soviet Union, military presence increases in Alaska.

1954 First wood-pulp mill in Alaska is completed at Ketchikan, giving a start to Alaska's large paper-producing industry.

1957 Oil is discovered on the Kenai Peninsula, making Alaska one of the world's most important oil-producing regions.

1959 Alaska becomes the forty-ninth state.

1964 A powerful earthquake strikes south central Alaska.

1971 Alaska Native Claims Settlement Act is passed.

1977 The Trans-Alaska Pipeline System, which transports oil from Prudhoe Bay to Valdez, is completed.

1980 Alaska National Interest Lands Conservation Act (ANILCA) is passed.

1989 *Exxon Valdez* supertanker spills 11 million gallons of crude oil into Prince William Sound.

1998 Voters pass an initiative that would make English the state's official language; district court overturns the measure as unconstitutional four years later.

2002 Voters defeat a plan to move the capital away from Juneau. A major earthquake rocks central Alaska and temporarily shuts down the oil pipeline.

2006 Augustine volcano in southwestern Alaska erupts.

ECONOMY

Agricultural Products: Barley, dairy products, grass seeds, livestock, potatoes

Dairy farm

Manufactured Products: Fish products, foodstuffs, gasoline, and petrochemicals

Natural Resources: Copper, forests, gold, lead, mercury, natural gas, oil, silver, tin, zinc

Business and Trade: Commercial fishing, forestry, fur trading, mining, tourism

CALENDAR OF CELEBRATIONS

Winter Sunrise After a long "night of darkness" from November to January, residents of Barrow are thrilled to see daylight again. The Winter Sunrise celebrates the welcome rays of the sun in late January.

Seward Polar Bear Jump Off Everyone probably likes jumping into a pool or lake to cool off during the hot days of summer, but this three-day event in January is not for the fainthearted. The main event of the Jump Off is a plunge into the frigid Resurrection Bay by the fearless members of the Polar Bear Club.

Fur Rendezvous Held in Anchorage in February, this ten-day carnival commemorates the fur trappers, who gathered in the city to sell their pelts and to socialize. During this celebration more than 140 events from sled dog races to snowshoe softball games take place.

Annual Alaska Folk Festival Musicians and music lovers alike come to Juneau in April to listen to concerts, attend workshops, and join in the various jam sessions. There are plenty of opportunities to dance as well as to listen to and perform music.

Fur Rendezvous

Iditarod Trail Sled Dog Race Also called the "Last Great Race on Earth," this popular competition runs from Anchorage to Nome. The Iditarod follows part of two former dog-team mail routes, one of which became newsworthy in 1925, when diphtheria serum was rushed to Nome and saved the city from an epidemic outbreak. The course runs almost 1,150 miles and has been declared a National Historic Trail.

Bering Sea Ice Golf Classic No experience in playing golf is needed to participate in this lighthearted event on the ice. This five-hole tournament in Nome helps wind up the last week of the Iditarod.

Kodiak Crab Festival The focus of this festival is the crab, one of Alaska's best-known seafoods, and the city's commercial fishing industry. It is held in Kodiak every year on Memorial Day weekend.

World Eskimo-Indian Olympics Held in Fairbanks in July, these games focus on Eskimo tradition and culture.

Alaska State Fair The annual fair in Palmer, held from late August through Labor Day, is a spectacular sight. It features legendary giant vegetables and nationally acclaimed fair gardens that yield over 20,000 flowers. There's plenty of family entertainment and delicious food for people of all ages to enjoy.

Bathtub Race You can win a statue of Miss Piggy and Kermit taking a bath by participating in this annual event in Nome. This unique race splashes off at noon on Labor Day. Five-member teams, one of whom must be in the bathtub, race bathtubs mounted on wheels down Front

Street. The rules state that the bathtub must be full of water at the beginning of the race and hold at least 10 gallons of water when it crosses the finish line.

STATE STARS

Aleksandr Baranov (1746–1819) was a Russian fur trader. He moved to Alaska in 1790 to run a fur-trading company that later became the Russian-American Company. The Russian-American Company governed the Russian colony in Alaska.

Edward Lewis Bartlett (1904–1968) was born in Seattle, Washington. His family relocated when he was one, and he grew up in Fairbanks, where he was an editor for the local newspaper from 1924 to 1933. In 1944 he was elected to represent Alaska in the U.S. Congress. Bartlett fought hard for Alaskan statehood.

Rex Beach (1877–1949) was a prominent writer associated with Alaska. Beach lived in Stevens Village and used this Alaskan town as the background for his book *The Barrier*. Another of Beach's books, *The Spoilers*, describes what Nome was like in its earlier days.

Vitus Bering (1681–1741), a Danish navigator, explored the continents of Asia and North America for Czar Peter the Great of Russia. On his first trip to northern Siberia, he concluded that the two continents were separated by water. During his 1741 expedition, Bering sighted Mount Saint Elias in Alaska. The trip ended sadly when heavy fog forced him to land on Bering Island, where he died of scurvy.

Susan Butcher (1954–) moved to Alaska from Cambridge, Massachusetts, in 1975 to raise sled dogs. In 1978 she competed in her first Iditarod Trail Sled Dog Race, finishing nineteenth. She kept racing and, in 1986 won the Iditarod in record time. In 1988 she became the first person to win three Iditarod races in a row. She won the race a fourth time in 1990.

Susan Butcher

Anthony Dimond (1881–1953) came to Alaska in 1904 as a prospector and miner. He started practicing law in Alaska in 1913 and later was a member of the Alaska Territorial Senate. Dimond served as mayor of Valdez for nine years. Dimond was a nonvoting delegate in the U.S. House of Representatives from 1932 to 1946.

William Egan (1914–1984) was born in Valdez, Alaska. He served as a member of the House of Representatives for the Alaska Territory and also as a one-term member of the Senate. In 1958 Egan was elected the first governor of the state of Alaska. He was reelected two times, in 1962 and 1970.

Carl Ben Eielson (1897–1929) came to Alaska in 1922 at the age of twenty-five. He became a bush pilot and, in 1928, was the first person to fly over the Arctic Ocean. Eielson died when his plane crashed during a rescue mission to help an icebound Russian ship.

Carl Ben Eielson

Ernest Gruening (1887–1974) introduced Alaska to the world through his books, which include *The State of Alaska* (1954) and *The Battle for Alaska Statehood* (1967). As a politician, he served Alaska in various positions from 1938 until 1969. In 1939 the U.S. Congress appointed Gruening as governor of the Alaska Territory.

Walter Hickel (1919–) is a businessperson and public official. In 1940 he moved to Alaska and founded the Hickel Construction Company. In 1966 he was elected the first Republican governor of Alaska. In 1990 he ran again for governor, that time as an Independent, and was elected.

Bernard R. Hubbard (1888–1962) was a Jesuit scientist and lecturer. Born in San Francisco, he made his first trip to Alaska in 1927 to explore its glaciers. He made ten other trips to Alaska during which he studied the language and customs of the Eskimos. He wrote two books: *Mush, You Malamutes* (1932) and *Cradle of the Storms* (1935).

Sheldon Jackson (1834–1909), educator and missionary, opened churches and schools across the country from 1859 to 1883. He did the same in Alaska in 1884. In 1891 he introduced reindeer to Alaska from their original habitats in northern Europe and Asia. These powerful animals were especially useful in the Arctic, where they could be trained to pull sleds through snow. Jackson served as the U.S. superintendent of public instruction in Alaska from 1885 to 1908.

Sydney Laurence (1865–1940), an artist born in Brooklyn, New York, often visited Alaska. Many of his paintings were of Native Americans and the Alaskan landscape. One of Laurence's paintings of Mount McKinley is displayed at the Smithsonian Institution in Washington, D.C.

Jack London (1876–1916) rose from poverty to become the most widely read novelist of his day. Eager for adventure, in 1897 he journeyed to the Yukon to participate in the gold rush. His Alaskan experiences show up in some of his writings, including the beloved *The Call of the Wild*. This novel is a fictional account of a Saint Bernard mix named Buck who was kidnapped from his California home to lead a pack of sled dogs during the Yukon gold rush.

Jack London

Elizabeth Wanamaker Peratrovich (1911–1958), a Native Alaskan, fought for Native rights in Alaska. As the president of Alaska Native Sisterhood, she struggled to win voting and civil rights for Native Alaskans. Her speech to the territorial legislature in 1945 regarding Native rights resulted in the passage of a law that banned discrimination against Natives.

Grigory Shelekov (1747–1795) was a Russian merchant and fur trader who founded Alaska's first trading post, on Kodiak Island in 1784.

Don Simpson (1945–1996) was a movie producer from Anchorage who worked on such hit films as *Top Gun*, *Flashdance*, and *Beverly Hills Cop*.

Father Ivan Veniaminov (1797–1879) worked for ten years among the Aleut peoples, learning their language and customs. Father Veniaminov translated parts of the Bible and several prayers and hymns into the Aleut language.

Sikvoan Weyahok (Howard Rock) (1911–1976) was born in Point Hope, Alaska. He was an Inupiaq painter and sculptor who, in 1962, founded the *Tundra Times* newspaper. That popular paper became the voice of Alaska's Native groups.

TOUR THE STATE

Inside Passage (southeastern coastal cities) The Inside Passage is the waterway for Alaska's state Marine Highway System. Ferry liners carry cars and passengers from Prince Rupert, British Columbia, and Seattle, Washington, to Alaska's southeastern coastal cities. In addition to the spectacular scenery, stops at towns along the route offer special attractions.

Ketchikan (south) Known as the Salmon Capital of the World, Ketchikan also has the world's largest collection of totem poles.

Ketchikan

Metlakatla (near Ketchikan) Visitors to this Tshimshian Indian village can also view a sawmill and a salmon cannery.

Sitka (south) A great number of Eastern Orthodox churches can be found in this city located on Alaska's scenic southeastern coast. The largest is Saint Michael's Cathedral, which contains many Russian religious paintings known as icons.

Sitka National Historical Park (near Sitka) This favorite visitors' destination is located on the edge of the historic city. Families can enjoy the wildlife sanctuary, a cultural center for Native American and Russian history, and a Tlingit totem pole park.

Juneau (southeast) Alaska's state government and its cultural hub are in the capital city of Juneau. The Alaska State Museum located there exhibits the most complete Eskimo art collection in the United States.

Mendenhall Glacier (north of Juneau) Visitors can land in a helicopter and walk on this magnificent glacier that measures twelve miles long and one and a half miles wide. Spectators can gaze down into the breathtakingly deep crevasses and cracks and, if thirsty, scoop a drink of water from a swift glacier stream.

Skagway (at the head of Lynn Canal) Step back in time to the exciting gold rush days! The city's seven-block boardwalk features shops and saloons that date from the gold rush or were built in the style of that period. Gold rush artifacts and Native cultural displays are on view at the granite Trail of '98 Museum.

Glacier Bay National Park (southeastern coast) Made a national park in 1925, it includes many enormous glaciers. Visitors also have opportunities to watch whales and seals at play.

Anchorage (southern coast) Anchorage is one of the state's most important cities. Over 40 percent of all Alaskans live there. In spite of its sprawl, Anchorage is only a short distance from some of the state's most beautiful natural scenery, such as glaciers, wildlife refuges, and Denali (formerly Mount McKinley).

Homer (southern coast) Many artists call this small town near the tip of the Kenai Peninsula home. Visitors can browse the art galleries, jewelry stores, and craft shops. Fishers from around the world come to Homer hoping to catch giant halibut.

Valdez (southern coast) This ice-free port is the southern terminus of the Trans-Alaska Pipeline. It also includes Columbia Glacier, Keystone Canyon, and Bridal Veil Falls. It is the site of the tragic *Exxon Valdez* oil spill of 1989.

Seward (on Resurrection Bay) This ice-free port is the gateway to the Kenai Peninsula and the interior of Alaska. The gathering place for big-game hunters, the city is named for secretary of state William Seward, who purchased Alaska for the United States from Russia in 1867.

Katmai National Park (on the Alaska Peninsula) The park is the home of the world's largest brown bears. In 1912 Mount Matmai erupted, leaving vents in the mountain's valley floor from which hot steam flows. This dramatic area, known as the Valley of Ten Thousand Smokes, is a favorite trek for hikers.

Katmai National Park

Kodiak (Kodiak Island) Visitors take a ferry to explore the state's oldest community and sixth-largest city. A wealth of Russian and Native artifacts can be found in the Baranov Museum, Alaska's oldest structure. The Eastern Orthodox Church, built in 1794, is Alaska's first church.

Nome (northern Alaska on the Bering Sea) This city is reachable only by air. Tourists can pan for gold in this historic gold rush town, or they can buy Eskimo clothing, jewelry, and carvings.

Kotzebue (western coast) One of the world's largest Eskimo villages, Inupiaq Eskimos make up 80 percent of its population. Many residents practice traditional subsistence lifestyles and use handmade fishing boats to make a living.

Point Barrow (northern Alaska) Point Barrow is the northernmost point in Alaska. Nearby is a memorial to the American actor and homespun humorist Will Rogers and his pilot, Wiley Post. Both died in a plane crash near Point Barrow in 1935.

The Arctic National Wildlife Refuge (northern Alaska) Although few visitors find their way to this wilderness area in the far northeast, this refuge is home to much of Alaska's abundant wildlife, including caribou, oxen, and migratory shorebirds.

Northern Lights (northern Alaska) The aurora borealis, or northern lights, is a waving, swirling curtain of color that stretches across the sky, occurring most frequently above 60 degrees north latitude. Alaska's residents and visitors never stop being fascinated by this beautiful sight.

FUN FACTS

Alaska's flag was designed by a thirteen-year-old boy.

America purchased Alaska for $7.2 million, or about two cents per acre.

Alaska's coastline, which measures 33,000 miles, is longer than the coastlines of all the other states combined.

Inland water in Alaska covers an area larger than the states of Vermont and New Hampshire combined.

On March 27, 1964, a massive earthquake, one of the most powerful ever recorded in North America, hit Alaska. In some parts of Anchorage, pavement fell thirty feet in just a few seconds.

Alaska has seven of the twenty highest mountain peaks in the United States, including Denali (Mount McKinley), which is the highest mountain peak in all of North America.

Find Out More

If you would like to find out more about Alaska, look in your school or public library, or in a book or a video store.

GENERAL STATE BOOKS

Johnston, Joyce. *Alaska*, 2nd edition. Minneapolis: Lerner Publications, 2001.

Somerville, Barbara. *Alaska*. New York: Children's Press, 2002.

BOOKS ABOUT ALASKAN PEOPLE, PLACES, OR HISTORY

Riddles, Libby. *Storm Run: The Story of the First Woman to Win the Iditarod Sled Dog Race*. Seattle: Sasquatch Books, 2001.

DVDS AND VIDEOS

Alaska's Whales and Wildlife. WonderVisions, 2004.

Building the Alaska Highway. PBS Home Video and DVD, 2005.

Denali: Alaska's Great Wilderness. PBS Home Video and DVD, 2005.

Discovering Alaska. Questar, Inc., 2001.

Glaciers: Alaska's Rivers of Ice. Wea Corp., 2003.

National Parks of Alaska. Image Entertainment, 2002.

Over Alaska. KCTS Television, 2001.

WEB SITES

The State of Alaska

www.state.ak.us

This is the official Web site of the state's government.

Alaska Facts and Information

www.state.ak.us/local/facts.shtml

This site offers students data, statistics, a student guide, and A to Z information on the state of Alaska.

Alaska Historical Society

www.alaskahistoricalsociety.org

The state historical society's Web site offers stories from Alaskan history and links to other sites.

Alaska

www.alaska.com

This is the Web site of the Anchorage *Daily News*, Alaska's most popular paper. It is a good place to find information about current events. The paper also sponsors the Alaskan Information Center.

Alaska Native Knowledge Network

www.ankn.uaf.edu

For information about Alaska's Native peoples, check the Web site of the Alaska Native Knowledge Network, a cooperative venture of tribal groups and universities.

Alaska Native Heritage Center

www.alaskanative.net

The Alaska Native Heritage Center celebrates Alaska's Native cultures.

Index

Page numbers in **boldface** are illustrations and charts.

agriculture, 92, 122, **123**
airplanes, 64–65, **65,** 106, 121
Alaska Highway, 48, 64, 111, 121
Alaskaland, 111
Alaska Marine Highway, 65
Alaska National Interest Lands Conservation Act (1980), 78–79, 83, 122
Alaska Native Claims Settlement Act (1971), 50, 57, 78, 122
Alaska Peninsula, 13, 14
Alaska Railroad, 65, 104, 105
Alaska Range, 14, 16
"Alaska's Flag" (state song), 116
Alaska State Fair, 126
alcoholism, 57
Aleutian Islands, 16, 47
Aleutian Range, 14
Aleut people, 9, 37, **37,** 39
Alutiiq people, 106
Anchorage, 33, 64, **104,** 104–105, 135
animals, 22, 28, **29,** 30–33, 71, 83, 115, 118, **119**
Arctic Circle, daylight in, 25
Arctic National Wildlife Refuge (ANWR), 82, 83-85, **84,** 108, 137
Arctic Ocean, 10, 18
Arctic Refuge: A Circle of Testimony, 85
arts and crafts, 36, 37, 69, 105, 130
Athabascan Indians, 36–37, 57

Baranov, Aleksandr, 41, **41,** 42, 127
Barrow, 25, 64, 108
Bartlett, Edward Lewis "Bob," 49, 127
Beach, Rex, 127
Benson, Benny, 85
Bering, Vitus, 39, 120, 127
Bering Sea, 11, 15

Bering Strait, 35, 53
birds, 30, 31, 32–33, 40, 102, 115, 118
boats, 37, 65, 66, 107
borders, state, 10–11, 117
boroughs, map of, 75
brain drain, 69
Bristol Bay, 107
Brooks Range, 17–18, 18
Buser, Martin, 71
Bush, George W., 82
Bush, the, 64
Butcher, Susan, 128, 128

cabin fever, 25–26
Call of the Wild (London), 131
Canada, 11, 48, 111
children, 58, 76
Christianity, 40, 62
Chugach Mountains, 14
Chukchi Sea, 11
cities and towns, 107, 133–135
    boroughs, 74
    far north region, 108
    interior region, 111
    population of, 33
    south central region, 103–105
    southeast region, 99, 101–102
    southwest region, 106–107
    See also specific cities
civil rights, 132
climate, 10, 20–22, 24–25, 117
clothing, 66
Coast Guard, 49
coastline, 9, 138
Coast Range, 13, 14
cold war, 48–49, 121
Coming into the Country (McPhee), 55
Congress, U.S., 46, 74, 121
Constitution, Alaskan, 48

construction industry, 89
Cook, James, 120
Cook Inlet, 14
Cook Inlet Region Native Corporation, 57
cost of living, 96–97
courts. *See* judicial branch
crafts. *See* arts and crafts
dance. *See* music and dance
daylight, amount of, 25–26, **26**
Degrees of Disaster (Wheelwright), 51
Denali (mountain), 10, **16**
Denali National Park, 22, 111, **112,** 121
Dimond, Anthony, 129
dogsleds, 64, 70–71

earthquakes, 10, 53, 122, 138
Eastern Orthodox Church, 40, 106, 137
economy, the, 53, 87–88, 122, 124
education, 58, 68–69
Egan, William, **49,** 129
Eielson, Carl Ben, 121, 129, **129**
elections, 74, 77, 78
employment, 53, 82, 87–88, **89,** 89–93, **94**
endangered species, 30–33, 118
English-only law, 77–78, 122
environmental issues, 30-33, 50–51, 78–79, 82–85, 91, 118
Eskimos. *See* Inupiaq people; Yupik people
ethnicities, **60,** 61–62
Ewan, Fred, 57, 81
executive branch, 73–74, 76
Exxon Valdez disaster, 50–51, 91, 122, 135

Fairbanks, 20, 27, 64, 111
far north region, 17–18, 108

federal government, 78–79, 80–81
ferries, 65, 107
festivals, 20, 25, 59, 95, 99, 105, 124–127
fishing industry, 46, 51, 87, 90–92, 121
flag, 85, **114,** 138
food, 37, 38–39, 57, 58, 63
fun facts, 138
fur trade, 39, 41, 120

gemstones, 115
geography, **12,** 13–18, 117
Glacier Bay National Park, 101, **102,** 135
glaciers, 10, 14, **15,** 22–24, **101,** 103–104
global warming, 22, 24–25
gold mining, 42–43, **43,** 93, 121
government, 46, 73–74, 76–79, 80–81, 89
governors, 6, 7, 25, **49,** 73–74, 129, 130
Great Depression, 46
Gruening, Ernest, 129
Gulf of Alaska, 10

Haida Indians, 36
Haines (town), 102
Hammond, Jay, 7
Harris, Richard, 42
health, Native Alaskans and, 39
Hickel, Walter, 6, 130
Homer (town), 105, 135
homesteading programs, 80
housing, 20, 38, 56
Hubbard, Bernard R., 130
Humane Society, U.S., 71
hunting, 6, 24, 38–39, 58

Iditarod Trail Sled Dog Race, 70–71, 126, 128
If You Lived Here, I'd Know Your Name (Lende), 6
immigrants, 55, 78
income, 97
Indians, 36–37
industry, 46, 82–84, 122, 124
    fishing industry, 46, 51, 87, 90–92, 121

lumber industry, 46, 53, 82–83, 121
oil industry, 50–51, 53, 83, 84, 87, 89, 108, 122
insects, 17, 33
Inside Passage. *See* southeast region
interior region, 16–17, 20, 21, 111
Internet, the, 96
Inupiaq people, 9, 37–38, 56, 137
Irving, Washington, 41

Jackson, Sheldon, 46, 130
judicial branch, 76, 78
Juneau, 42, 53, 101, 122, 134
Juneau, Joe, 42

Kaiyuh Mountains, 16
Katmai National Park, 14–15, 106–107, 135, **136**
kayaks, 66, **66**
Kenai Fjords National Park, 105
Kenai Mountains, 14
Kenai Peninsula, 14
Kennecott Copper Mine, 103
Ketchikan (town), 99, 133, **133**
Klondike gold rush, 42–43
Klondike Gold Rush National Historical Park, 102
"Klondike Gold Rush" (song), 44–45
Knowles, Tony, 25
Kobuk Valley National Park, 108, **109**
Kodiak Island, 15, 106, **106**
Kodiak (town), 137
Kotzebue (town), 137
Kuskokwim Mountains, 16
Kuskokwim River, 15

Lake Illiamna, 15
lakes and rivers, 15, 17, **17,** 78–79, 117, 138
land ownership, 78–81, 82–85
landscape, 17, 18, 20, 111
languages, 9, 58, 62, 77–78, 122
Laurence, Sydney, 130
law enforcement, 49
legislative branch, 46, 74, 76, 77
London, Jack, 130–131, **131**
lumber industry, 46, 53, 82–83, 121
manufactured products, 124

maps
    Alaska by Road, **2**
    boroughs, **75**
    employment, **94**
    geography, **12**
    places to see, **110**
    population, **67**
McPhee, John, 55
Mendenhall Glacier, 101, 134
mental health, 57
Metlakatla (town), 134
military presence, 47–48, 49, 121
mining, 42–43, 46, 53, 89, 93, 121
motto, 115
mountains, 10, 13, 14, 16, 17–18, 138
Mount Marathon, 105
Mount Pavlof, 14
Mt. McKinley. *See* Denali
Muir, John, 6, 27
Murkowski, Frank H., **74**
museums, 101, 105, 106, 108, 111, 134, 137
music and dance, 44–45, 58, 101, 116, 124
muskeg, 17

name, origin of, 9, 115
national parks
    Denali National Park, 22, 111, **112,** 121
    Glacier Bay National Park, 101, **102,** 135
    Katmai National Park, 14–15, 106–107, 135, **136**
    Kenai Fjords National Park, 105
    Klondike Gold Rush National Historical Park, 102
    Kobuk Valley National Park, 108, **109**
    Sitka National Historical Park, 134
    Wrangell–Saint Elias National Park, 7, 10, 80–81, 81, 103, 103
National Park Service, 80–81, 111
National Wildlife Federation, 80
Native Alaskans, 35–39, 36, 56, 56–59, 92–93
    Alaska Native Claims Settlement Act (1971), 50, 57, 78, 122

Arctic National Wildlife Refuge (ANWR) and, 85
civil rights for, 132
English-only law and, 78
global warming and, 24
Iditarod Trail Sled Dog Race and, 71
inventions of, 66
religion of, 40
settlement of Alaska and, 120
traditions of, 6, 7, 99
natural resources, 87, 89, 124
New Anchorage, 41, 42
New Angel Dancers, 101
Nome, 25, 43, 108, 137
northern lights, 27, **27,** 137
North Slope, 18, 21, 108

oil industry, 50–51, 53, 83–84, 87, 89, 91, 108, 122
oil spills, 50–51, **51,** 91
Old Harbor (town), 106
Oomingmak Musk Ox Producer's Co-op, 105
out-migration, 69

Pacific Ocean, 10
Panhandle. *See* southeast region
Peratrovich, Elizabeth Wanamaker, 132
permafrost, 18, 20, 24
Permanent Fund dividend, 97
Petersburg (town), 99
places to see, map of, **110**
plants and flowers, 18, 22, 30, 115, 118
Point Barrow, 137
population
    cities and towns, 53, **107**
    density of, 33
    ethnicities, **60,** 61–62
    growth of, **52,** 55
    map of, **67**
    Native Alaskan, 56–59
    oil industry and, 51
poverty, 92–93, 97
Prince William Sound, 14, 51
Prudhoe Bay, 50
purchase of Alaska, 42, 120, 138

radar stations, 48–49

railroads, 46, 65
Ray Mountains, 16
recipes, smoked salmon, 63
recreation, 69, 70–71
    See also festivals
Red Devil (town), 33
regions, 13–18, 20, 99, 101–108
religion, 40, 62, 132
risks, of Alaska, 6
rivers. *See* lakes and rivers
roads, 64, 104–105
Russia, 10, 39–42, 48, 52–53, 106, 120
Russian-American Company, 40–41, 127
Russian culture, 101

Saint Elias Mountains, 14
sand dunes, 108
sea ice, 22, 24
seal, Alaskan, **114**
Seal Hunters (Brown), 38
settlement, of Alaska, 35, 38, 39–42, 99, 120
Seward, William, 42, **42,** 120, 135
Seward Peninsula, 17
Seward (town), 105, 135
Shelekov, Grigory, 132
Shishmaref (town), 6, 24
shopping, 96
Simpson, Don, 132
Sitka National Historical Park, 134
Sitka (town), 41, 101, 134
size, of Alaska, 6, 10
Skagway (town), 43, 102, 134
skiing, 70
snowmobiles, 64, **65**
south central region, 14, 103–105
southeast region, **13,** 13–14, 21, 99, 101–102, 132
southwest region, 14–16, 106-107
sports, 69, 105, 126
"starring," tradition of, 40
state capital, 53, 101, 122
state fairs, 95, 126
statehood, 48, 122
state product, 96, 124
state song, 116
Steller, Georg, 39
Sundown, Mary Ann, 7, 56

Talkeetna Mountains, 14
taxes, 53
timeline, 120–122
Tlingit Indians, 36, 41, **58**
Tongass National Forest, 10, 82–83, **83**
totem poles, 99, **100**
tourism, 14, 71, 84–85, 87, 90, 99, 103, 106
traditions, Native Alaskan, 40, 56, 57, 58, 59
Trans-Alaska Pipeline, 49, 50, **50,** 122, 135
transportation, 6, 46, 48, 52–53, 64–65
Travels in Alaska (Muir), 6
Tshimshian Indians, 36
tundra, 18, **19,** 20
Tundra Times (newspaper), 132

universities, 68, 69
U.S. English (organization), 78

Valdez (town), 135
Valley of Ten Thousand Smokes, 106–107, 135
Vancouver, George, 120
Veniaminov, Ivan, 120, 132
volcanoes, 10, 14–15, 106–107, 122, 135

Weyahok, Sikvoan, 132
Wheelwright, Jeff, 51
White Mountains, 16
wildlife. *See* animals; plants and flowers
wildlife refuges, 78, 80
winds, 21
Wood-Tikchik State Park, 10
woodworking, 36
World War II, 46–48, 121
Worthington Glacier, **15**
Wrangell Mountains, 14
Wrangell-Saint Elias National Park, 7, 10, 80–81, **81, 103,** 103
writers, 127, 129, 130, 130–131

Young, Samuel Hall, 46
Yukon River, 15, 17, **17**
Yupik people, 37–38, 56, 108

ABOUT THE AUTHOR

Rebecca Stefoff is the author of numerous books for young readers, including several other volumes in the Celebrate the States series. Many of her books are about the exploration, settling, and history of the American West. Stefoff has written briefly about Alaska in *Growth in America: 1865–1914*, part of her North American Historical Atlases series, published by Benchmark Books. She welcomed this book as a chance to write at greater length about the biggest American state. Stefoff lives in Portland, Oregon. You can learn more about her and her books at her Web site, www.rebeccastefoff.com.